Contributions to Management Science

The series *Contributions to Management Science* contains research publications in all fields of business and management science. These publications are primarily monographs and multiple author works containing new research results, and also feature selected conference-based publications are also considered. The focus of the series lies in presenting the development of latest theoretical and empirical research across different viewpoints.

This book series is indexed in Scopus.

Erik Busch · Klaus Henning Busch ·
Volker Heyse · Kai Nobach

Methodology of Innovation

Basic Arithmetic of Creative Problem Solving

Springer

Erik Busch
Siemens Healthineers AG
Forchheim, Germany

Klaus Henning Busch
itf Innovationstransfer- und
Forschungsinstitut Schwerin e. V.
Schwerin, Germany

Volker Heyse
Heyse-Stiftung Menschenbilder –
Menschenbildung
Donaustauf, Germany

Kai Nobach
Ohm Technical University of Applied
Sciences
Nuremberg, Germany

ISSN 1431-1941 ISSN 2197-716X (electronic)
Contributions to Management Science
ISBN 978-3-658-50009-2 ISBN 978-3-658-50010-8 (eBook)
https://doi.org/10.1007/978-3-658-50010-8

This book is a translation of the original German edition "Methodik der Innovation," 2nd edition, by Erik Busch et al., published by Springer Fachmedien Wiesbaden GmbH in 2024. The translation was done with the help of an artificial intelligence machine translation tool. A subsequent human revision was done primarily in terms of content, so that the book will read stylistically differently from a conventional translation. Springer Nature works continuously to further the development of tools for the production of books and on the related technologies to support the authors.

This Springer imprint is published by the registered company Springer Fachmedien Wiesbaden GmbH, part of Springer Nature.
The registered company address is: Abraham-Lincoln-Str. 46, 65189 Wiesbaden, Germany

Preface

To motivate you to read this book, we tell the story of a factory in China, where soap is produced and packed in boxes.

The packaging process in this factory is flawed, so some boxes do not contain a soap bar. This naturally leads to customer complaints. The factory director therefore commissions two engineering teams to find a solution and build a prototype.

The first team comes from the highly developed East/North of China, the second from the less developed West of China.

Team 1	Team 2
Uses the latest technology available on the market Using laser beams, the vibration of the soap boxes on the conveyor belt is determined and from these data – using a very fast computer – the content is inferred To ensure the result is very accurate, a redundant system is connected in parallel. This determines the content of the box using radar Subsequently, the boxes that are supposed to be empty are marked and removed from the belt by a robot (see Fig. 1) The solution is quite expensive and the learning algorithms will need time and perhaps software updates to become very accurate	Places a fan next to the conveyor belt This blows the empty boxes away

Here fiction ends, and reality begins. After the amusing and entertaining side of this story fades, some may ask themselves: "What can I learn from this sbn tory?" (see Fig. 1).

- This example illustrates how essential the search for solution variants is for business success.
- Variation is one of the fundamental methods of innovation.
- Innovation does not necessarily have to be associated with costly investments.

This book describes the basic methodology for innovative action and explains it using examples from medical engineering and other industries. It also addresses other important aspects of successful innovation.

Fig. 1 Alternative solution possibilities. (Busch et al. 2021)

Why should you follow the explanations of these very authors?

The authors involved in this book are a multidisciplinary team that has been intensively involved with innovation processes for a long time and examines them from different perspectives. We would now like to introduce ourselves briefly, as this is a prerequisite for the success of a joint project or even for having just an interesting conversation.

	**Dr. Erik Busch** is familiar with the challenges of IT startups and global medical engineering providers. He has analyzed market and customer needs in Europe, the USA, and Asia, translated these requirements into innovative products, and then marketed them in such a way that they sustainably increase brand value and business results
	**Prof. Dr. sc. Klaus Henning Busch** acquired the foundations for his professional activity in mechanical engineering and pedagogy studies at the Technical University of Dresden. After his assistantship and the development of veterinary medical research technology, he switched to educational research. His specialties are in innovation methodology and professional development

Prof. Dr. Volker Heyse
is the managing partner of several human resources development consulting companies (ACT SKoM GmbH, CeKom GmbH, AdRem) and founding rector of the state-recognized private University of Applied Sciences for SMEs (FHM) Bielefeld. He teaches in the field of competence and strength development in Germany and abroad and is the author and editor of numerous books

Prof. Dr. Dr. h. c. Kai Nobach
is a full professor at the Ohm Technical University of Applied Sciences Nuremberg and a management consultant and trainer. He has been intensively involved in methods of innovation and project management in practice, research, and teaching for many years and teaches in Germany and abroad. His main focus is on management control systems for innovation activities and project management control

Now that you have met the stakeholders involved in the creation of this book, we would like to introduce you as well. After all, you are our partner as a reader and our collaborator in working with this material.

We do not (yet) know you personally. However, we already know quite a bit about you.

We are sure that you are a student, teacher, artist, engineer, business economist, manager, and/or you are interested in developing and implementing original ideas. You can do this with enthusiasm and may have already dealt with literature on creativity.

Therefore, we have a common basis for further work with the present material.

First, we should agree on a common **objective** for working with this material.

With this book, we want to provide a **learning and working material** that supports you in developing new original solutions and successfully implementing innovations.

You should also experience some excitement and enjoyment and ultimately achieve the desired and necessary successes.

These successes should benefit both you and your company, as well as be useful to the general public.

Now the question is how we want to achieve this common goal — specifically **the path to the goal**.

The emergence of new solutions in technology, business, medicine, art, politics, the military, and everyday life was and still is often shrouded in the fog of inspiration.

Experienced practitioners, scientists, and even "creativity present an almost unmanageable number of methods for developing and implementing creative ideas. This immense variety of methods and numerous recipes result in a complexity problem in practice.

In contrast to some innovation methods, concepts in other knowledge areas consist of a few elements that are then combined, e.g.

- Mathematics with ten Arabic numerals and four basic arithmetic operations,
- Modern music theory with seven notes and time signatures,
- Color theory with the five primary hues of the Munsell color system,
- Culinary arts with five flavors, and
- The theory of the Five Phases (五行) with its five elements.

However, creative work has increasingly grown out of the stage of "alchemy". We therefore ask ourselves:

Can creative and innovative work—the inventing—also be based on a few basic arithmetic operations?

"There are no more than five musical notes, yet the combinations of these five create more melodies than can ever be heard.

There are no more than five primary colors, yet combined they produce more shades than can ever be seen.

There are no more than five flavors—sour, spicy, salty, sweet, and bitter -, yet their combinations create more flavors than can ever be tasted." Sun Tzu (孫子), The Art of War (Sun Tzu, 1988, p. 45 f.)

This book aims to show that the five basic operations of creative problem solving

—Specification, Dialogue, Analogy, Combination, and Variation—

and their combinations can be used for comprehensive creative work.

Furthermore, it will demonstrate how developed ideas can be successfully implemented—from invention to innovation—and the fundamental importance of communication and the conveyance of innovation competencies for innovation processes. Moreover, it will illustrate how innovation processes can be effectively managed and controlled from a business management perspective.

Let's walk this path together!

Let's tackle it together!

Literatur

- Busch, E., Bulitta, C., Nobach, K., & Strobel, N. (2021). Innovation & Entwicklung im globalen Wettbewerb. *MED engineering*, *4*, 56–58. https://med-eng.de/2021/10/28/innovation/
- Sun Tzu. (1988). *The Art of War*. Knaur.

Hemhofen, Germany — Erik Busch
Rostock, Germany — Klaus Henning Busch
Donaustauf, Germany — Volker Heyse
Nuremberg, Germany — Kai Nobach
Summer 2025

Contents

1 Fundamentals of Innovative Thinking and Acting 1
1.1 Definition of Creativity Rules 2
1.1.1 First Creativity Rule................................ 2
1.1.2 Second Creativity Rule 3
1.1.3 Third Creativity Rule................................ 3
1.1.4 Fourth Creativity Rule 3
1.1.5 Fifth Creativity Rule 4
1.2 Sensitizing for Innovative Problem Situations................. 10
1.3 Relevance of Innovations from a Business Perspective.......... 16
1.4 Definition and Characteristics of Innovations 17
1.5 Motivation for Implementing Innovation Activities 19
1.6 Types of Innovations from an Economic Perspective 20
1.7 Analysis of Innovation Needs and Realization of Innovation Potentials 24
References.. 28

2 Efficient Methods for Identifying Innovative Problems 31
2.1 Selection and Application of Suitable Methods................ 31
2.2 System Analysis.. 32
2.3 The Portfolio Technique.................................... 36
2.4 The Envelope Curve Technique............................. 39
2.5 The Delphi Technique 41
2.6 The Scenario Technique.................................... 43
2.7 The Process Analysis...................................... 45
2.8 The Product Line Analysis.................................. 46
References.. 46

3 Diagnosis of the Problem Situation.............................. 49
3.1 System Analytical Perspective............................... 49
3.2 Identifying and Analyzing Contradictions..................... 56
References.. 57

4 Developing Solution Ideas 59
4.1 Diversity of Methods 59
4.2 Identifying Analogies 61
4.2.1 Introductory Remarks 61
4.2.2 Inspiration from Adjacent Fields 61
4.2.3 Inspiration from Nature 62
4.2.4 Inspiration from Historical Sources 62
4.3 Adaptation of Abstract Solution Ideas 69
4.3.1 Introductory Remarks 69
4.3.2 Concretization through Variation 69
4.3.3 Concretization by Combining 75
References 77

5 Communication in the Innovation Process 79
5.1 The Central Role of Dialogue 79
5.2 The Central and Supporting Element in the Invention Process 80
5.3 Basics of Communication 83
5.4 Efficient Communication Methods in the Innovation Process 84
5.5 The Particular Effectiveness of Creative Groups 85
References 110

6 From Invention to Innovation 111
6.1 Goal Orientation and Will to Succeed 112
6.2 Management Control of Innovation Activities 114
6.2.1 Objectives and Tasks of Innovation Management Control 115
6.2.2 Levels of Management Control of Innovation Activities 117
6.2.3 Control Systems to Manage Innovation at Corporate and Portfolio Level 119
6.2.4 Requirements for Managing Innovation Activities at Project Level 124
6.2.5 Management Control Tools for Traditionally Managed Innovation Projects 125
6.2.6 Management Control Tools for Agile Managed Innovation Projects 133
6.3 Securing Intellectual Property 139
6.4 Appropriate Preparation of the Invention for Transfer 142
6.4.1 Testing of Functional Models 142
6.4.2 Product Approval 142
6.5 Implementation and Distribution 148
6.5.1 From Manufacturing to Application 148
6.5.2 Developing the Distribution Strategy 149
6.6 Acquiring and Teaching of Innovation Competence 149
6.6.1 Lifelong Acquisition of Innovation Competence 149
6.6.2 Integrated Project Delivery of Innovation Competence 154

6.7 Implementing the Innovation Methodology 159
6.7.1 Fields of Innovation 159
6.7.2 Distribution Paths for Successful Use of the Methodology 160
6.7.3 Promoting the Use of Innovation Methodology. 162
References. 164

7 **Afterword**. 169

List of Figures

Fig. 1.1 Positioning of patients on the operating table. (Adapted from Busch, 2021) . . . 6
Fig. 1.2 Contradictions for the Example Patient Support . . . 6
Fig. 1.3 Basic methods in the invention triangle. (Adapted from Busch et al., 2021a, b) . . . 8
Fig. 1.4 The methods as a springboard for overcoming mental barriers. (Busch, 1976) . . . 10
Fig. 1.5 Ranking of impulse generators in the innovation and development process. (After Busch et al., 2021a, b) . . . 11
Fig. 1.6 Classification of problem situations . . . 14
Fig. 1.7 Problem cube. (Adapted from Busch & Busch, 1980) . . . 15
Fig. 1.8 Iterative developments in the product life cycle . . . 15
Fig. 1.9 Framework conditions for innovations in a VUCA-BANI world . . . 16
Fig. 1.10 Key characteristics and targets of innovation . . . 18
Fig. 1.11 Economic reasons for corporate innovation activities . . . 20
Fig. 1.12 Alternative approaches to systematizing innovations . . . 21
Fig. 1.13 Potential methods and tools for analyzing innovation needs . . . 25
Fig. 2.1 MediGuide Technology—Use of symbolic overlay on EKG and breath-synchronized X-ray series . . . 33
Fig. 2.2 IT Infrastructure of Interventional Laboratories. (Adapted from Busch, 2003) . . . 34
Fig. 2.3 Modular computer structure. (Adapted from Busch, 2003) . . . 36
Fig. 2.4 Portfolio Matrix . . . 38
Fig. 2.5 Development curves . . . 40
Fig. 2.6 Scenario Technique . . . 44
Fig. 3.1 Scheme for preparing problem statements . . . 50
Fig. 3.2 Guideline for preparing problem statements for the development of technical solutions presented . . . 51
Fig. 3.3 Operators and operations in process analysis . . . 52
Fig. 3.4 Analysis of the "Embryo Transfer" system in a simplified representation . . . 54

Fig. 3.5 An example of interdisciplinary development work, from left to right: Dr. med. Claus Christmann, Prof. Dr. Klaus Henning Busch, Dr. rer. nat. Klaus-Jürgen Kurth 55
Fig. 4.1 Approach to problem-solving using the analogy method 63
Fig. 4.2 Originality of analogies depending on the level of abstraction and the analogy area 66
Fig. 4.3 Hypothetical schema of the analogy 68
Fig. 4.4 Possibilities for qualitative modifications 70
Fig. 4.5 Variation possibilities. (After K. H. Busch, 1985, p. 61). 71
Fig. 4.6 Variations for supporting blood flow. 72
Fig. 4.7 Signal cables during rotational angiography 73
Fig. 4.8 Variation table 74
Fig. 4.9 Cable holder in the angiography lab 75
Fig. 4.10 Combination possibilities. (Busch, 1985, p. 68) 76
Fig. 5.1 Position of dialogue in the invention process. (Adapted from Busch et al., 2021) 80
Fig. 5.2 Sketch for the desired "shaking device" 81
Fig. 5.3 Sender-and-Receiver Model 83
Fig. 5.4 Correlation between the rankings of the test subjects and the actual surface area. Number of deviations from the real values approaching zero 100
Fig. 5.5 The ctc faculty in front of the Bauhaus in Dessau. 108
Fig. 5.6 Seminar in a ctc course 109
Fig. 6.1 Levels of measuring and controlling innovation activities 118
Fig. 6.2 Effective tools to measure and control innovation activities 119
Fig. 6.3 Tools for analyzing the benefit and value of innovation initiatives 121
Fig. 6.4 Methods for calculating the economic value of an innovation project 122
Fig. 6.5 Basic elements of traditional project planning 125
Fig. 6.6 Documentation and reporting tools for innovation risks 127
Fig. 6.7 Examples of a Milestone and Cost Trend Analysis 128
Fig. 6.8 Example of a Time/Cost Trend Diagram. 128
Fig. 6.9 Calculation example for an Earned Value Analysis. 130
Fig. 6.10 Examples of report formats in project reporting 132
Fig. 6.11 Example of a Function Point Curve and a Burndown Chart 134
Fig. 6.12 Example of a Burnup Chart to control the overall project progress 135
Fig. 6.13 Specific metrics to control agile managed innovation projects. 136
Fig. 6.14 Protective rights strategies depending on the level of invention and market development 140
Fig. 6.15 Product Lifecycle. 140

Fig. 6.16 Innovation and development process. (Adapted from Busch, 2021) 144
Fig. 6.17 Implementation and Distribution 148
Fig. 6.18 Learning and working in the phases of the innovation process 156

1
Fundamentals of Innovative Thinking and Acting

Abstract As children, we often played: I spy with my little eye something that is red (or blue). This game sharpens attention and also aids in recognizing and naming colors. A few years later, one could also play: I see something that you see too—and what we see could be done differently (or better). This game stimulates imagination and makes it clear that not everything is optimal and that some things could be done differently or better. It trains—initially hidden and unconsciously—the ability to recognize areas for improvement. It fosters and trains the personality trait of problem sensitivity—and thus forms the basis for innovative thinking and action. In this chapter, we focus on the recognition of problems, the underlying contradictions, and provide an overview of the approaches suitable for solving the identified problems. First, we provide you with ten rules that convey important experiences and simultaneously encourage you to successfully navigate the obstacle course from problem identification to its solution. On this journey, you will not be spared from resolving contradictions. But you have already encountered this principle when listening to and reading fairy tales. You are thus in the role of the brave knight or the clever farmer's daughter. In this chapter, you will also learn that the "toolbox" of the problem solver consists of a few methods and behaviors. Just as mathematics manages with a few basic arithmetic operations, there is also a manageable "set of building blocks" which includes the analogy method, the variation method, the combination method, and—as a connecting element—communication. Not every difficult situation has to be a problem. We therefore distinguish between problems and tasks that can be solved with subject-specific knowledge, and we highlight the distinguishing features of problems and tasks. It is important to accept that the recognition of the need for innovation and thus the stimuli for new solutions can come not only from the technical field, but also particularly from economics, medicine, biology, and all areas of life. Studies in the field of medical technology also show that the initiators of innovations come from all stages of the innovation process. These include users (e.g., medical staff), sales, service, product management, and staff involved in development. In Chap. 3 some

E. Busch et al., *Methodology of Innovation*, Contributions to Management Science,
https://doi.org/10.1007/978-3-658-50010-8_1

proven methods are presented that can rationally shape the recognition of problems described here.

1.1 Definition of Creativity Rules

Since the time when the Greeks applauded the performances of tragedies, it has been customary to precede the actual work with a prologue. Even today, in film and television, the prologue serves to introduce the content to be presented. It provides harmonious information about the idea of the material, the motivation, and the goals.

Similarly, the overture has an introductory and opening function at the beginning of concerts, operas, or some plays. The overture is usually structured in three parts and can contain typical elements of the plot as well as hints about the characters and their character. The main motifs and melodies are introduced.

In this book, we will follow these traditions and present proven behaviors and rules as well as a brief introductory example in this harmonious section. Some important terms such as analogy, adaptation, diagnosis, and transfer will also be explained. In addition, the basics of innovation economics will be presented.

We follow Lohmann and Luther, who attached special importance to the explanation of terms and norms.

Lohmann demanded in his methodology lecture: First the child—and then the baptism. (So first a description and then the naming.) (Lohmann, 1960)

The reformer Martin Luther provided an explanation for each of the Ten Commandments with "What is this?" (Luther, 1950)

So let's start with some rules that can be useful when working out creative solutions.

1.1.1 First Creativity Rule

Every day, several people left the house and stumbled over a brick left lying on the ground after a few meters.

The first person did not mind much. She continued as if nothing had happened.

The second person stumbled and cursed about this mess—but walked briskly on.

The third person stumbled—and simply pushed the culprit aside.

The fourth person picked up the stone—and thought about how she could use it.

What do we learn from this different behavior?

Important **Develop your problem sensitivity! Every recognized problem is an opportunity for a beneficial solution!**

1.1.2 Second Creativity Rule

The story told in the preface about the soap factory is a good example of this. After the amusing and entertaining side of this story has faded, we remember the second creativity rule:

Important **Always strive for the surprisingly simple!**

1.1.3 Third Creativity Rule

In the Gotha Engineering Office for Mechanization, a machine for making ice lollies was to be developed and manufactured (Linde, 1988).

The problem: During the freezing process, the ice—due to expansion—pressed firmly against the wall and therefore could not be easily removed from the casting mold.

The molds were then made conical or pyramidal designed so that the ice pushed itself out of the casting mold due to expansion.

We note the third creativity rule:

Important **Aim for solutions where the problem solves itself!**

1.1.4 Fourth Creativity Rule

There are many regions worldwide where the demand for meat—especially high-quality meat—cannot be met even today. For millennia, it has been common to use male domestic animals both as work animals and for human consumption. To do this, they are often "deprived of their masculinity" at an early age. However, a difficulty arises.

Male animals have a good increase in high-quality muscle meat and they have better feed conversion than female animals. On the other hand, male animals have a particular odor and taste intensity due to their pheromones and testosterone, which is not compatible with eating habits in many regions.

So if the male young animals intended for fattening are castrated shortly after birth (at the latest by the fifth day of life)—as usual—they do not grow as well as female animals or untreated male animals.

However, if the animals are castrated only twelve weeks before slaughter, the meat loses its intense smell and taste; however, the health problems for the animals due to this procedure are considerable. The accumulated meat mass is partially lost again.

This contradiction had to be solved by an original idea.

One possibility suggested was to implant a device at a young age that would then be "ignited" at the appropriate age.

A second variant proposed performing the procedure twelve weeks before the slaughter date through minimally invasive surgery.

We derive the following creativity rule:

Important Identify the main contradiction at the core of the problem and solve the problem!

1.1.5 Fifth Creativity Rule

Since about 1820, work has been done in several countries on the production of light by electric current. Patents were already granted in 1845, 1852, and 1854 (Conrad, 1980).

Joseph Swan developed a light bulb from 1860, and in 1878 he succeeded in developing the first usable electric light bulb.

Edison improved Swan's light bulb. The improvement to up to 1000 h of light duration took another three years of development time.

(König, 1997)

The following story is told about this. When Edison was told after numerous failed attempts: "The project has failed." He is said to have replied: "We didn't fail. Now I know a thousand ways not to make an incandescent lamp."

(brainyquote.com, 2021)

After their success, Swan and Edison founded the joint company Ediswan.

What do we learn from this development process?

Important The inventor who continues to work when others have already given up is successful! An invention only becomes effective when it has established itself as an innovation in the market!

As promised above, we want to turn to a **simple example** in this introduction that can demonstrate the characteristic features of the creative process in a short form.

Example
In interventions using both minimally invasive methods (e.g., catheter or endoscopy techniques) and conventional surgical techniques, stable and comfortable patient positioning is essential, see Fig. 1.1.
In the process of their work, the medical staff identified some opportunities for improvement or further development of the operating tables. The physicians were thus the initiators of the development work.
The following problems were identified:

- In particular, the safe positioning of heavy patients is currently associated with high risk, as the securing of the apron is usually done with belts, straps, or similar. Due to their small area—compared to the volume held—patient comfort is low.
- The heat management to prevent patients from cooling down is either realized by insulating materials—which do not allow active heat management—or by heat-emitting pads—which absorb X-rays and thus affect image quality.
- To prevent decubitus by distributing the pressure load, not sufficient procedures have been implemented in the OR area so far. This is particularly due to the difficulty of repositioning in the sterile area where the patient is during the operation.
- The weight recording and the recording of vital data prove to be inadequate.
- The mechanical fixation is improper.
- The patient monitoring is not optimal.
- The adjustment of the bed height to the table height is problematic. There can be gaps between the movable patient bed and patient table.

The task is currently made more difficult by the increasing number of overweight people—and thus obese patients. Since 1980, their number has almost doubled. This trend must also be taken into account in the development of biomedical devices. ◄

From the named problems, several **contradictions** become apparent. Examples are shown in Fig. 1.2.

The identified problems and contradictions were introduced into the company's organization by the medical staff through sales—who simultaneously act as initiators and liaisons.

For those in **Product Lifecycle Management (PLM)—as problem solvers—** the following **development task** was formulated:

"Develop a device for positioning patients on examination and operating tables".

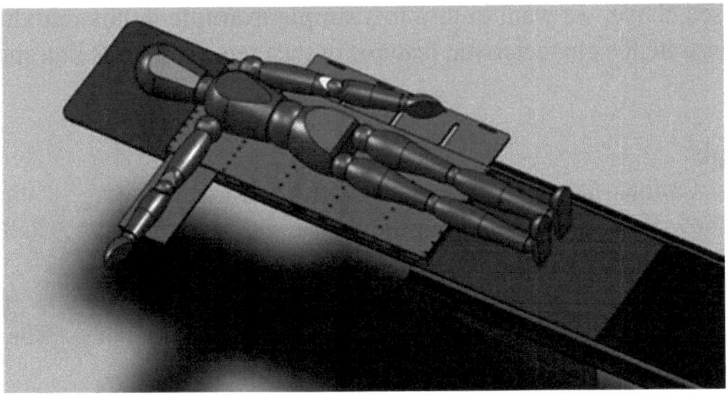

Fig. 1.1 Positioning of patients on the operating table. (Adapted from Busch, 2021)

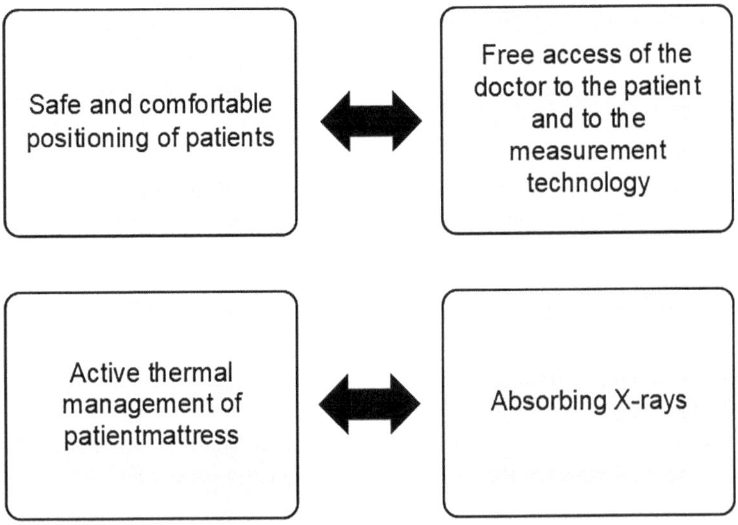

Fig. 1.2 Contradictions for the Example Patient Support

In diagnosing the problem situation—especially with regard to procedures in the cardiac catheterization laboratory—the following requirements for the solution to be achieved were defined, among others:

- Change of patient positioning for the purpose of improved doctor's access to the areas of the body to be treated
- Optimal pressure relief—means for surface enlargement
- Radiolucent design
- Minimization of wrinkling to prevent pressure sores Isolation from electrical currents

- Heat retaining
- Hygienic and quick to clean with surface disinfection
- Low material and maintenance costs

The complex problem was initially broken down into several sub-problems:

- Patient fixation
- Adjustment of bed height to the operating table
- Patient transfer
- Patient monitoring
- Recording of vital signs
- Special requirements for obese patients

In specifying the problem and in the search for solution ideas, the **communication between the involved parties**, i.e. the medical staff, the sales staff, the service and the development engineers, was initially in the foreground. The dialogue remained the central element in the entire creative process and is also a crucial element in customer care and marketing as a continuous contact.

The development work to solve the problems began with the **identification of analogies**.

For the participants, **remembering** similar solutions in analogous problem situations provided an "entry" into the collection of ideas. Similar, already existing technical solutions were given priority.

Since no ready-made solution could be adopted, suggestions had to be sought at a higher level of abstraction. The following **analogies** came to mind for the employees: extendable table, forklift and lifting platform.

From these concrete suggestions, the core of the solution idea had to be first raised to an **abstract level** in order to then adapt the principle of action again at a concrete level **to the given conditions and demands.**

The mentioned work steps—see Fig. 1.3—are realized by the following methodical means for the development of solution variants:

- the analogy method,
- the variation method,
- the combination method, and
- the dialog method.

The identification of variants is based on intuitive and systematic approaches.

The **analogy method** is based on remembering similarities and transferring them to the current situation.

With the **variation method**, improved, further developed or novel solution possibilities are derived from an existing solution through targeted, systematic changes. The variation requires a structural analysis. Changes to all system properties can be considered, including individual elements, their couplings and arrangements, as well as the function and environment of the system.

In addition to quantitative modifications, variation operations particularly involve qualitative changes through:

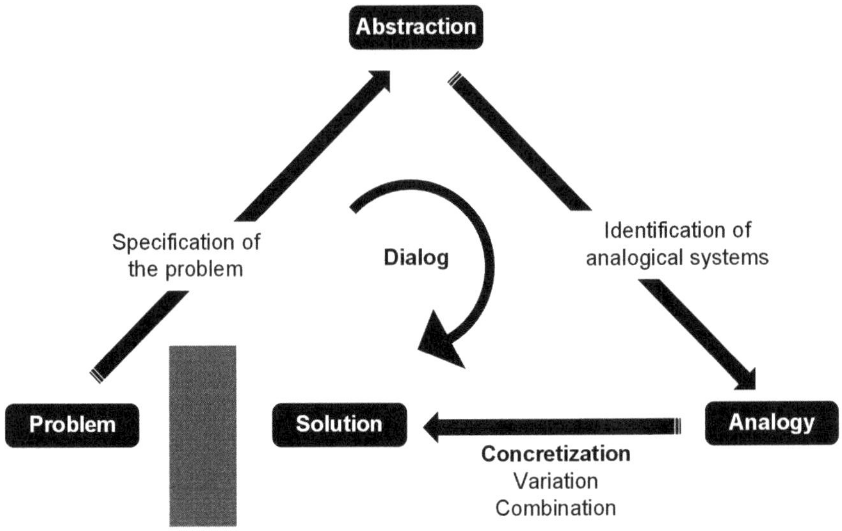

Fig. 1.3 Basic methods in the invention triangle. (Adapted from Busch et al., 2021a, b)

- Replacement,
- Addition,
- Omission,
- Decomposition,
- Consolidation, and
- Reversal

are possible.

The **combination method** builds on variation. Realization variants are determined for the variables. These variants are then fully or partially related to each other (to be combined). The combination table and the combination matrix are common forms of representation. The matrix representation allows the individual fields to be viewed in their context and to mark preferred variants.

The **dialog method** (brainstorming, brainwriting, braindesign) uses association chains to initiate the linking of ideas, concepts, and other features from a starting situation. The dialogue is conducted in various forms during the variant search. In addition to discussion, experience transfer in workshops, conferences, and seminars, brainstorming has become widely spread.

The result of the solution search usually presents several alternative solution variants, the further processing of which needs to be decided. The identified ideas need to be evaluated to select the most favorable variant(s).

While an invention provides an idea, an innovation includes successful implementation in practice, including marketing (see Sect. 1.3).

An innovation is thus a novelty resulting from human work, reflecting a leap in quality in a development process. The new quality is generally the result of solving a contradiction.

Example

In the present example, the development resulted in the blocking publication "Extended functions for increased patient safety in angiography systems". The following result is presented in excerpt:

"A combination of various individual components greatly improves the safety of the patient on the angiography table.

The integration of weight sensors in the table allows for a quick and precise recording of the current patient weight.

The essential aspect of this invention is the integration of sensors for weight measurement. In the recording of the table top there are sensors for pressure and thus weight detection. Pressure sensors are integrated on the opposite side of the projection/ledge from the table top in the base. The table top now rests on the sensors, and no longer on the table mount in the base.

Calibration of the sensors to the individual table tops with different weight and geometry is done in the same way as the table top recognition using the positioning pins. Each plate has a different number or geometry of positioning pins and can thus be clearly identified by the table base. This ensures that only the patient's weight is recorded, even with different table tops.

Since the sensors are safety-relevant components, they are redundant, i.e. designed at least twice. In the event of a sensor or processing unit failure, the system continues to operate unchanged. A corresponding message about the failure of components can be issued and measures for repair initiated.

The measured value is recorded via a free interface with the processing hardware and processed using suitable software. A direct entry into the patient protocol and the display on the monitors is done. ...

A further execution of this invention consists in the extension of the angiography table using sensors for the detection of weight differences on the table top. Pressure sensors are used for this purpose in the lateral support surfaces in the table base." (Busch et al., 2009)

With the successful realization of the solution, the problem-solving process was completed. ◄

With this prologue, we aimed to introduce our approach to problem-solving and explain some of the terms and behaviors used.

We generally face a problem when there is an inadequacy or difficult situation to be resolved, or when a desire needs to be fulfilled and we do not (yet) have a (or a sufficient) solution.

Before us stands (figuratively speaking) a mental barrier—a wall that we need to overcome (see Fig. 1.4).

Heinrich Busch (Busch, 1976) sketched this in the following image, simultaneously illustrating that a "springboard" is very useful for overcoming the barrier.

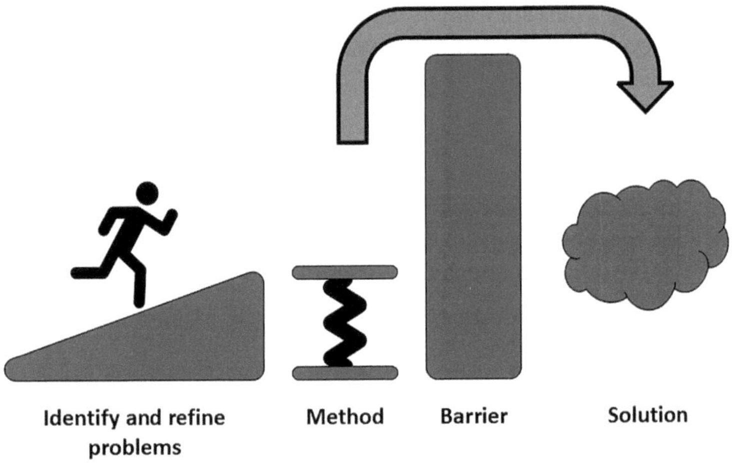

Fig. 1.4 The methods as a springboard for overcoming mental barriers. (Busch, 1976)

In the following sections, we want to deal more closely with the individual phases of the problem-solving process.

1.2 Sensitizing for Innovative Problem Situations

The sources for original ideas are diverse and multifaceted. The following four examples are intended to highlight some of these peculiarities.

In the course of the investigations on the "Development of biomedical devices with a large and durable base and the associated services" (Busch et al., 2021a, b), the following ranking of impulse generators for new and further developments was shown (see Fig. 1.5):

- sales with 53%,
- the customers/users with 28%,
- product management with 7%,
- service with 5%,
- customer relationship management with 4% and
- competition with 3%.

These impulse generators are important for the market-oriented control of innovation and development activities in the company.

As part of a forward-looking **company management** and especially of management control, the market development, international patent activities, crisis situations, sustainability aspects and increasing digitalization are observed and analyzed. From this, particularly from a business economics perspective, innovation strategies for the own company are derived (see Sect. 1.3 and 1.5).

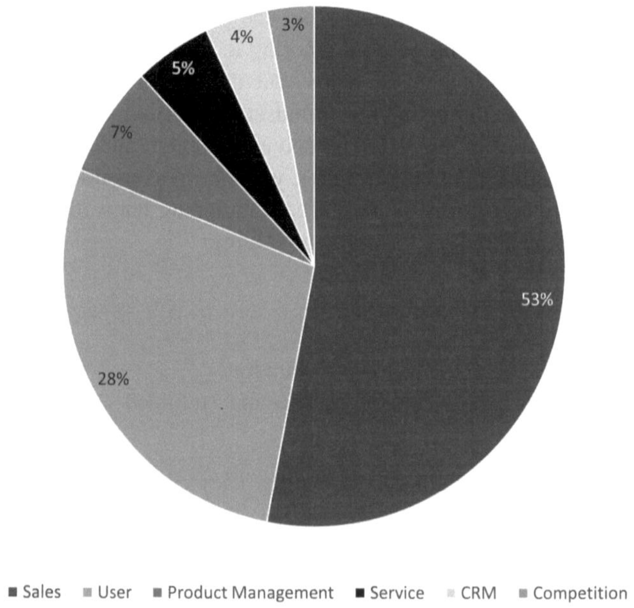

Fig. 1.5 Ranking of impulse generators in the innovation and development process. (After Busch et al., 2021a, b)

Within the framework of the **Employee Suggestion Scheme**, all employees of a company have the opportunity to submit their ideas for improving products, work tools, organizational solutions, and accident prevention.

In the **personal environment**, in club life and in the wider social environment, ideas emerge to change existing technical, design or organizational conditions. These changes—as far as they are desired and possible—can be realized either independently or as an external service.

These examples have in common that in the individual cognition process for identifying innovative problem situations, extensive information processing with multiple filters and amplifiers takes place.

The basis for developing one's own activities is initially the subjective perception of a deviation from an expected value. The actual characteristics (parameters) of an objectively existing system (or a process) deviate from the subjectively desired or objectively required target state.

In this perception, objectively existing stimuli of the sensory organs are converted into subjectively experienced sensations.

This process includes an ad-hoc evaluation, which is determined by the respective attitudes, subjective norms, and behavioral orientations.

Both the scope and urgency of remedying the situation have an influence. This is evident, among other things, in behavior during disasters and accidents compared to long-term predictable development projects.

The sensations and their evaluations are the prerequisite for the triggering of action impulses. These can range from ignoring to creative responding.

The awareness of problem situations and the resulting action impulses are influenced by goal orientation, interest, mindset, motivation, and emotions.

The personality trait required for perceiving problem and contradiction situations as well as improvement opportunities, we refer to as **problem sensitivity**.

This personality trait forms the basis for recognizing innovation-promoting situations and initiating activities for problem-solving.

Example
To illustrate, let's recall the following situation:
Every day, several people left the house and stumbled after a few meters over a leftover brick.

- The first person was not bothered by this. They continued as if nothing had happened.
- The second person stumbled and grumbled about this mess—but quickly moved on.
- The third person stumbled—and simply pushed the culprit aside.
- The fourth person picked up the stone—and thought about how she could use it. ◀

Depending on whether a solution path is already known for the solution of the recognized situation, or whether a procedure must be newly developed, we distinguish between task and problem.

A **problem** characterizes the "*knowledge of an individual or a group of people that the mastered knowledge is not sufficient to achieve a goal required by practice, and that this knowledge therefore needs to be expanded accordingly.*

In a narrower sense, the knowledge of such a knowledge deficit is only called a 'problem' when

- *the missing knowledge cannot be taken over by other members of society, but must be newly developed,*
- *and no algorithm is known by which the identified knowledge deficit can be remedied in a finite number of steps that can also be carried out.*" (Klaus & Buhr, 1976)

A **task** exists when a solution path is known.

The conscious recognition and formulation of problems are generally dependent on the character traits, motives, abilities, and skills of people.

The following prerequisites promote the recognition of problem situations:

- Motivation to improve existing situations and structures
- Questioning "proven" solutions

- Recognition of contradictions
- Knowledge about the laws of the development of technical and social systems
- Knowledge of the international status and trends in one's own and adjacent fields of expertise, including patent literature
- Knowledge about the weaknesses and strengths of the considered system
- Transfer of knowledge from other fields to one's own field of work
- General knowledge, interest, and openness

Heinrich Busch (Busch, 1976) proposed a classification of problem situations.

Figure 1.6 explains individual classes of problem situations.

A dichotomous (binary) division of information into "available" and "not available" rarely characterizes the existing situation.

Additional information often needs to be obtained for the initial situation (input).

For the solution path (process), a general procedure may be known, but it needs to be adapted to the specific conditions of the task.

For the required result (output), specific parameters often need to be determined and agreed upon within the scope of a specification.

Therefore, if the situation is treated as a continuous variable (e.g., from 0 to 1), it can be represented as a problem cube (see Fig. 1.7).

In the **development of biomedical devices** with a large and long-lasting base and the associated services, there are—similar to motor vehicles and software products—peculiarities that can be represented in the product life cycle. Existing (outdated) product components are replaced with further developments or new functional elements are added. This can "stretch" the decline phase or initiate a new life cycle (see Fig. 1.8).

The iterative partial developments particularly refer to the following in the present cases:

- the application,
- the mechanics,
- the device interfaces,
- the user interfaces, and
- the electronics.

The type of interventions mainly involved:

- repairs (similar replacement),
- detail improvements,
- additions, and
- updates.

In the period between the acquisition and the end of use of the devices, the clinical, technical, and economic environment changes. This potential for change is fed from various sources of innovation. (MCDonald & Brown, 1994)

An **innovation and development process that takes these relevant sources of innovation into account** and thus anticipates changes in the clinical, technical, and economic environment can produce products and services that better serve market needs. (Vahs & Burmester, 2005)

The biomedical devices used have a life cycle of about 8 years and a high purchase price. (Lee, 2014)

Participation in the above-mentioned development through the optimization of clinically, operationally, or financially relevant properties during the life cycle is therefore financially more attractive than new acquisition or complete

Initial Situation	Solution Path Process	Goal Result	Remarks
known	**known**	**known**	There is **no problem,** but a trivial transformation **task** with a given algorithm.
unknown	**known**	**known**	There is **no problem,** but a **task**. The required result can be achieved using a known procedure.
known	*unknown*	**known**	There is **a problem.** A process is to be developed from a given initial state (input) to a desired target state (output). (Process development)
known	**known**	*unknown*	**A task** exists because the solution path is known. A (unknown) target state is to be determined from a given input using a given method.
unknown	*unknown*	**known**	There is **a problem.** A procedure and suitable initial situation must be determined for a required result.
known	*unknown*	*unknown*	There is **a problem.** New methods need to be developed that enable meaningful results from existing initial states.
unknown	**known**	*unknown*	New areas of application (application possibilities) are to be determined for a given process. (means-purpose connection)

Fig. 1.6 Classification of problem situations

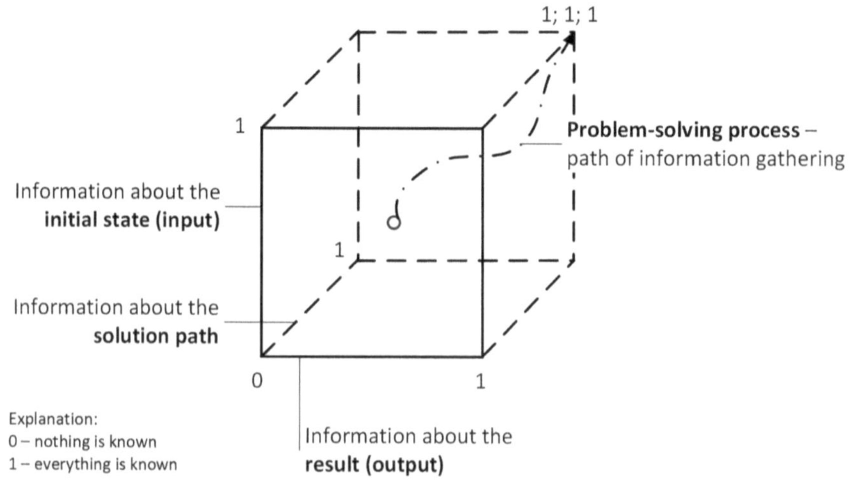

Fig. 1.7 Problem cube. (Adapted from Busch & Busch, 1980)

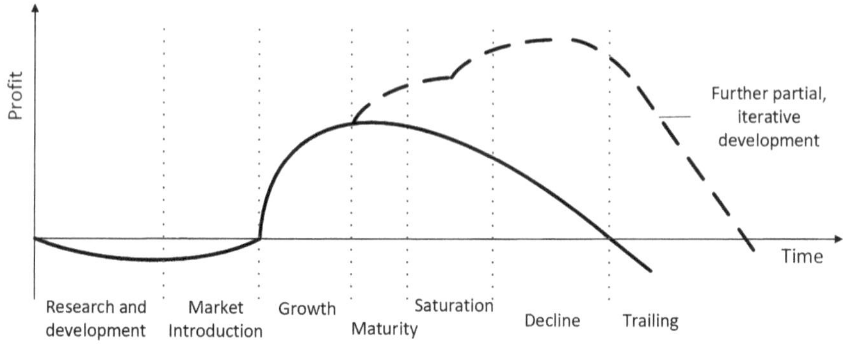

Fig. 1.8 Iterative developments in the product life cycle

replacement. (Brooks, 2017; Ryckx et al., 2016; Sferrella, 2019; Siemens Healthineers, 2024)

This results in the motivation for the iterative development of these biomedical devices. This requires the design of the **innovation and development process as a control loop**. (Busch et al., 2021a, b)

This finding proves that innovation processes are by no means purely technical matters, but always involve the **unity of business management and invention** to be considered.

This connection is the subject of **innovation economics**.

Important!
Innovation economics is a sub-discipline of economics.
It deals with the interconnections between inventions and business economics. In particular, it examines the conditions for the emergence of innovations and their establishment in the market, as well as their macroeconomic aspects and regional and global effects (Grupp, 1997; Innovation Economics, 2022).

1.3 Relevance of Innovations from a Business Perspective

In a world characterized by volatility, uncertainty, complexity, and ambiguity (VUCA environment), companies must act quickly and flexibly to respond appropriately to market changes and other challenges. This applies in particular with regard to the individualization of customer desires, networking of value chains, digitalization and agility, as well as crisis situations and sustainability aspects. Therefore, management is called upon to constantly review the business models and value creation structures and **initiate innovative changes early on** (see Fig. 1.9).

Background, Additional Information
This adaptability will play an even more important role in the future, as companies due to current developments (climate change, Covid-19 pandemic, energy crisis etc.) must adapt to an environment that can be described with the attributes “brittle”, “anxious”, “non-linear” and

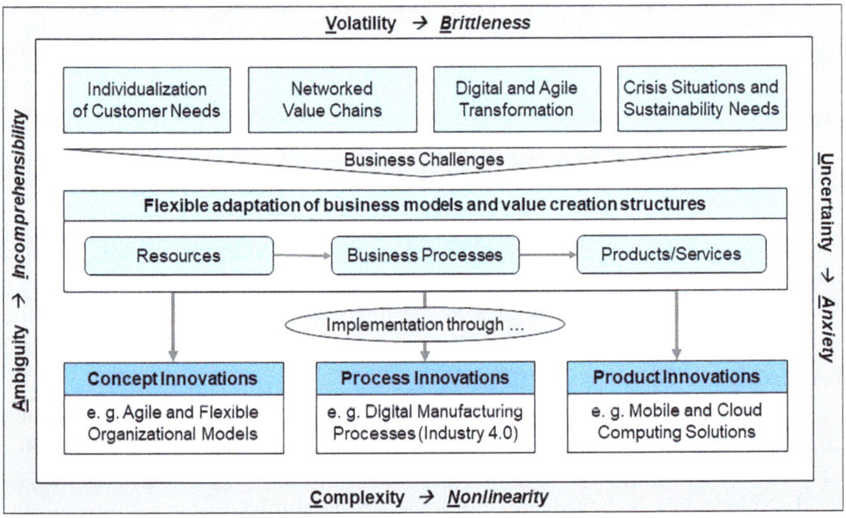

Fig. 1.9 Framework conditions for innovations in a VUCA-BANI world

"incomprehensible" (BANI) according to the American futurist Jamais Cascio (Cascio, 2020). In this **VUCA-BANI world**, it is of central importance to systematically build up and realize new potential for success, as this is the only way to ensure the company's long-term existence. To do this, innovation opportunities must be continuously identified and implemented. If the company has the necessary competencies for this, it is generally considered to be capable of **innovation** (Landwehr-Zloch, 2022).

Innovative corporate action is usually triggered by technology-driven, political and sustainability-related factors and, in particular, by demand aspects and other economic constraints. With reference to the economic requirements, the characteristics and relevance of innovations are considered below from a business perspective and approaches for identifying and implementing innovation potentials are discussed. The following questions will be addressed in detail:

Overview

- What characteristics do innovations have from a business perspective?
- Where does the motivation for innovation come from in companies?
- What types of innovations can be distinguished from an economic perspective?
- How can innovation potentials be systematically analyzed and implemented?

1.4 Definition and Characteristics of Innovations

In economics, innovations are generally understood as **(complex) novelties** that are associated with technological, societal, and economic change (Möhrle & Specht, 2018). From a business perspective, innovations represent the introduction or changes of products, processes, or resources that provide the company with competitive advantages and growth opportunities (Schuh & Bender, 2012). The actual benefit or value of an innovation is often only recognizable after a longer period of time. The benefits can be derived from financial, ecological, or social aspects in terms of **sustainability** (for the importance of sustainability in innovation management see (Nelke, 2016)).

Looking at the phases of the innovation process, Schumpeter distinguishes between the terms **invention, innovation, and diffusion** (Schumpeter, 1961). An **invention** refers to a new concept, product, or process that has been developed or researched based on a creative idea. An **innovation** only exists when the **invention** has economic potential and is specifically implemented in the market or in business processes. The market launch or application of a new problem solution is therefore considered an innovation in the narrower sense. The term **diffusion** finally describes the general spread of the innovation in the market or among users. The speed of diffusion of the innovation depends on the frequency of adoption by market participants or users.

Practically speaking, innovation can be defined as follows (Weis, 2022):

Definition Innovation = Creative Idea + Invention + Diffusion

In addition to these general criteria, **other characteristics** can be used to characterize innovations from a business perspective. This is significant insofar as the manifestations of these characteristics influence the achievement of the desired innovation goals and thus affect the economic success of the company (see Fig. 1.10).

Crucial for the success of innovation are **three levels of requirements**, which can be described with a model common in business management:

Important! The magic triangle of time, quality, and budget.

In terms of **time**, innovations need to be initiated **as early as possible** and implemented quickly to generate competitive advantages. For example, in product development, a short time-to-use can achieve higher market success (Landwehr-Zloch, 2022). The **quality of innovation** processes depends on how well customer needs are met and to what extent the innovation creates a **unique selling point** in the sense of a "Unique Selling Proposition (USP)". The **innovation budget** includes the available physical, personnel, technological, and financial resources for the development and implementation of the innovation. The **financial budget** for process or concept innovations must only reflect the expected costs or payments to be made for the innovation work. For market-oriented product innovations, the budget must also include targets for market shares, sales revenues, and cash flow.

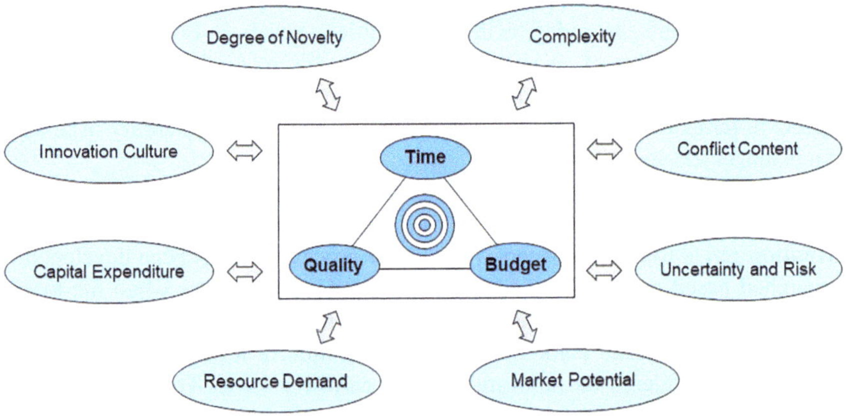

Fig. 1.10 Key characteristics and targets of innovation

The dimensions of time, quality, and budget are influenced by numerous factors that result from the **specific characteristics of innovations**. These include the **degree of novelty** and market potential as well as the **conflict content** and the company-specific innovation culture and resource situation. In addition, innovation activities are often associated with high complexity and are always associated with **uncertainty**.

Important! Therefore, innovation activities always involve risks.

Innovation risks can result from resource scarcity, technical implementation difficulties, marketing problems, or a lack of willingness to innovate. The extent of these risks often affects the targets for the financing costs and the payback period of the innovation project (for the assessment of innovation risks, see (Granig, 2007)).

1.5 Motivation for Implementing Innovation Activities

Economically speaking, the search for new, preferably unique business ideas and the development of previously unknown solutions for existing problems plays a central role in **ensuring future competitiveness**, addressing growth issues, responding to sustainability requirements, and satisfying the interests of capital investors. This can be seen, for example, in the high research and development expenditures of innovative companies (Stifterverband, 2022) and in meaningful company publications on innovation activities and results (Landwehr-Zloch, 2022).

The motivation for companies to innovate lies in the fact that promising innovations can sustainably **secure the company's existence** and increase its **economic success** (Schäperkötter, 2022). The goal is to strengthen their competitive position by developing innovative problem solutions and to achieve financial targets while considering ecological and social aspects.

Important! From an economic perspective, innovation projects aim primarily to increase **profitability**, ensure **solvency**, and sustainably increase the **company value** (see Fig. 1.11).

Innovative companies regularly search for optimization potentials and creative solutions for resources, processes and products/services in order to generate **strategic competitive advantages** in terms of time, quality, and cost, and to increase operational efficiency (Weis, 2022).

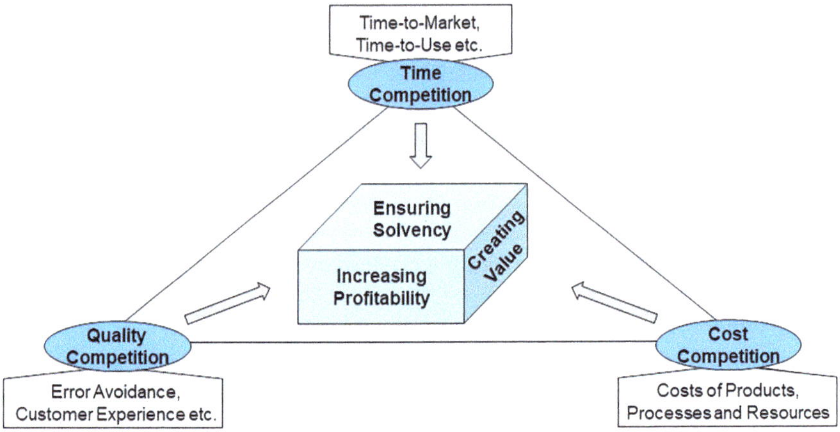

Fig. 1.11 Economic reasons for corporate innovation activities

Overview

If companies succeed in effectively implementing innovative ideas by utilizing their own and/or external potentials, they can achieve market success, realize cash flows, and then reinvest these in the **maintenance and expansion** of their innovation capabilities. Therefore, management must ensure that this **economic cycle** is continuously initiated and maintained through innovation activities, especially in a rapidly changing environment (Landwehr-Zloch, 2022). In business, the development of new products and services is particularly important, as it often offers the opportunity to achieve higher margins than with the further development of established products. Moreover, the **innovation of entire business models** plays a central role in generating strategic competitive advantages, as this can achieve returns that are sometimes many times higher than with product or process innovations (Fibitz, 2019).

1.6 Types of Innovations from an Economic Perspective

Background, Additional Information

While the relevance of innovations for achieving economic success is undisputed in theory and practice, the question of when a novelty is considered an innovation is a controversial one. The **understanding of innovation** ranges from the development of a new type of application with no significant external impact to disruptive innovations that radically change existing business models and market constellations as "game changers". Disruptive business model innovations are often triggered or enabled by new digital technologies (Michel, 2017).

Considering the **broad interpretability of the concept of innovation**, various approaches have been developed in science and practice to systematize innovations, aiming to enable targeted innovation management.

Overview

Based on the business understanding of innovation activity, four basic **systematization approaches** can be used to categorizing innovations and deriving the relevant target sizes, task fields, and methods of innovation control in the respective context (see Fig. 1.12).

If one focuses on the **output** of company-specific innovation activity, it can initially be differentiated whether the innovation results in a change in the sales program or an optimization of internal processes, structures, and organizational concepts. If the innovation leads to a successful market launch of a new product or service, it is referred to as a **product or service innovation**.

If, on the other hand, the innovative action results in a temporal, qualitative, or cost-related improvement of the internal resources and processes, it is a **process or infrastructure innovation** (Gemünden & Littkemann, 2007). The innovation performance can also consist of developing a new business model or a novel approach of management or organizational structure (Kaschny et al., 2015). Such innovations can be summarized under the term **concept innovation**.

Another differentiation criterion for innovation performance can be the **degree of innovation** (Schuh & Bender, 2012). This allows for the distinction between incremental innovations with a low degree of innovation (e.g., expansion of storage capacity in mobile communication devices) and radical innovations with a high degree of innovation (e.g., invention of the iPhone). This distinction is particularly important because **projects with radical innovation content** must be managed differently than projects that only aim for incremental innovations (K. Möller et al., 2016). In the case of radical innovation projects, particular

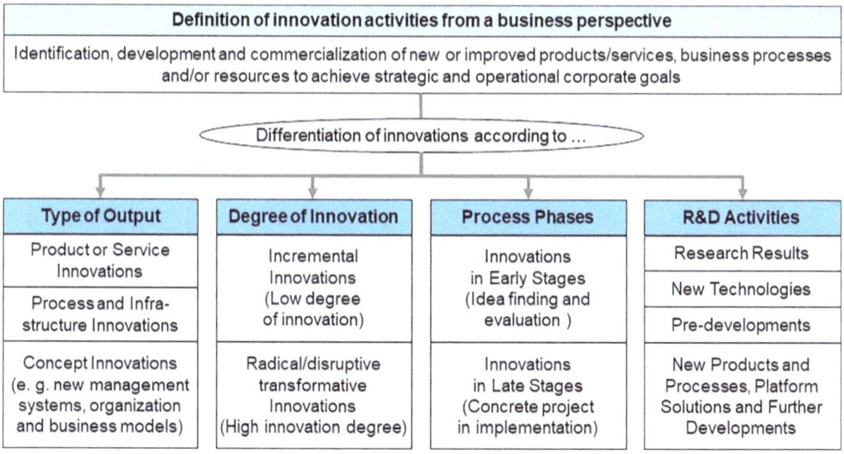

Fig. 1.12 Alternative approaches to systematizing innovations

attention must be paid to allowing project members to manage innovation activities autonomously and flexibly. In this context, the **speed of innovation** also plays a crucial role, as higher degrees of innovation are often achieved by companies that recognize new market requirements early and respond quickly (Meyer, 2016).

From a **process perspective**, innovation projects can be differentiated according to the phase of the innovation life cycle they are in. The range extends from identified innovation opportunities in the early stage of idea generation to innovations in the planning and conception phase to concrete development projects with a clearly defined business case. Innovation projects in the early phases are characterized in particular by uncertainty regarding technical feasibility and later value contribution. In projects in the implementation phase, on the other hand, uncertainty often decreases due to learning effects, while complexity increases due to the growing number of actors to be coordinated (Landwehr-Zloch, 2022).

As a fourth systematization approach, innovations can finally be divided according to ideal-typical **activities** and results in the field of **research and development (R&D)**. The general acquisition of new knowledge in the form of research results, technological novelties, or preliminary developments on the one hand is to be distinguished from the concrete application-oriented (further) development of new products, processes, or platform solutions on the other hand.

Important! From a market and value creation perspective, the **output-oriented approach and the differentiation** according to typical **R&D activities** are particularly suitable for systematically identifying innovation potentials and consistently managing innovations.

From an output-oriented perspective, innovation projects can generally be differentiated according to whether they relate to **products and services, business processes**, used **resources**, or entire **business models**. For further investigation, potentials and measures for redesigning company-specific value creation are therefore divided into business model, product, process, and resource innovations.

Business model innovations can relate to the value proposition for customers as well as the company-specific value creation dimension and/or the revenue model (Fibitz, 2019).

Example

With regard to customer relationships, the introduction and expansion of **online trading** is considered a far-reaching business model innovation, as digital sales platforms now represent a significant distribution pillar in almost every industry. From a product perspective, business model innovations have led to **digital companies** like Apple, Google, and Facebook or service providers like Uber and Airbnb (Michel, 2017). The latter put established companies under considerable pressure by providing services without having to maintain capital-intensive resources such as vehicles or buildings themselves. ◀

From a structural perspective, **product innovations** can refer to the core product, the product design, or product-specific additional services. The development of innovative products in many industries is primarily driven by the availability of new digital technologies. This is evident in car manufacturers, for example, who regularly need to innovatively adapt their product range due to trends such as autonomous driving,

e-mobility, and vehicle networking. In terms of the revenues to be generated in the market with products or services, technical novelties also open up the use of innovative **pricing models**.

Example
The aircraft turbine manufacturer Rolls Royce introduced a so-called **"Pay-per-Use" concept** for its customers years ago, where the aircraft operators pay a fee for each operating hour of the engine instead of buying it themselves. To implement this concept, engine data is collected centrally and evaluated using sensors (Nobach, 2019). ◀

Process innovations are changes in operational workflows through redesign, automation, digitization, outsourcing, and other measures aimed at using resources for business activities more efficiently (Schallmo & Brecht, 2017). This includes concepts of **Industry 4.0**, which enable companies to identify new cause-and-effect relationships, uncover inefficiencies, and digitize processes. By innovatively using these potentials, cross-functional and cross-company **value creation networks** can also be established to streamline, speed up, and reduce the cost of business processes (Kaschny et al., 2015).

Example
In production, the **networking of workpieces and manufacturing robots** using modern sensor technology can help optimize processing sequences and reduce plant failures (Rusch et al., 2016). Moreover, approaches to artificial intelligence and robotic solutions offer further innovation possibilities that can also be used for the automation of administrative processes (e. g., automated recording and booking of invoices in accounting departments). ◀

Resource innovations include the invention and implementation of new input factors for existing or future business processes (e.g., new resources, technologies, knowledge potentials, types of financing, and information systems) as well as new solutions for provision, sizing and utilization of capacities (e.g., innovative contract design, in-/outsourcing, and new concepts for resource management).

Example

The innovative **exploitation of new input factors** includes the much-discussed use of hydrogen as an energy carrier for industrial and fuel cell applications. In the context of capacity provision and utilization, innovations can be achieved by networking the value creation system using Industry 4.0 approaches. For instance, companies can use the production data transmitted via machine-to-machine communication in a **Smart Factory** to optimize capacity sizing and utilization control. In terms of resource provision, innovative action can also involve entering into strategic partnerships or investing in other companies to gain access to key resources that have not been or are not sufficiently available. (Nobach, 2019). ◄

1.7 Analysis of Innovation Needs and Realization of Innovation Potentials

For a structured analysis of innovation needs and the systematic implementation of identified innovation potentials, various procedural models have been developed in theory and practice, which essentially include the following **process steps**:

Important!

1. Analysis of the environment (opportunities and risks) and the company (strengths and weaknesses)
2. Problem definition and goal setting (innovation needs)
3. Idea generation and evaluation (innovation potentials)
4. Prioritization and selection of innovation candidates
5. Development, creation, and marketing of selected innovation projects

The first step is to **systematically analyze** the external conditions and economic megatrends in the company-specific market and competitive environment. The strategic management's range of methods offers suitable tools for this, such as the PESTEL analysis, Porter's industry structure model, or McKinsey's 7-S model (Baum et al., 2013). The challenges identified (market developments, growth expectations, technology changes, consumer trends, etc.) usually motivate management to take innovative paths. Farsighted managers will therefore actively look for new customer needs, application fields for technologies, innovative service offerings, and other **market opportunities**. Based on the market conditions, the company's internal structures and processes must then be examined to identify both optimization needs and opportunities to **build on the company's own strengths**.

> **Overview**
> For a systematic **derivation of innovation needs**, it is useful to differentiate between products or services, processes, and resources already in the analysis phase. With a view to the innovation-related target sizes of time, quality, and cost, as well as the market-specific influencing factors, different **approaches and tools** can be used (see Fig. 1.13).

From a **product perspective**, the first step is to analyze customer satisfaction and needs to identify starting points for improving or redesigning product functions or ideas for new product developments. In addition, the available product technologies and the product-specific development, creation, and marketing times must be examined and evaluated. From a monetary perspective, innovation needs can be derived from the analysis of current and potential **revenue and payment models and cost structures**. With a view to marketing, sales financing and processing customer payments, it can be examined, for example, whether usage-based pricing models (e.g., Pay per Use, Software as a Service), innovative financing models

<table>
<tr><th>Analytical Approaches</th><th>Products/Services</th><th>Business Processes</th><th>Resources</th></tr>
<tr><td rowspan="2">Technology-oriented</td><td></td><td colspan="2">Technology Portfolio Analysis</td></tr>
<tr><td colspan="3">Technology Balance Sheet</td></tr>
<tr><td rowspan="3">Cost-based</td><td colspan="3">Technology Cost Analysis</td></tr>
<tr><td colspan="3">Life Cycle Cost Analysis, Total Cost of Ownership</td></tr>
<tr><td>Target Costing</td><td>Activity Based Costing</td><td>Resource Cost Analysis</td></tr>
<tr><td>Time-related</td><td colspan="2">Development Cycle and Time to Market Analysis</td><td></td></tr>
<tr><td rowspan="3">Customer-oriented</td><td colspan="2">Customer Requirements/Satisfaction Analysis</td><td></td></tr>
<tr><td>Lead User Method</td><td></td><td></td></tr>
<tr><td rowspan="3">Crowd Sourcing / Open Innnovation</td><td></td><td></td></tr>
<tr><td>Supplier-oriented</td><td colspan="2">Delivery Time and Availability Analysis</td></tr>
<tr><td>Employee-related</td><td></td><td>Employee Survey</td></tr>
<tr><td>Competition-oriented</td><td colspan="3">Benchmarking</td></tr>
</table>

Fig. 1.13 Potential methods and tools for analyzing innovation needs

(e.g., Finetrading), or digital payment solutions should be developed and offered. For the identification of product-specific cost reduction potentials, concepts such as **Target Costing** can be used (Horváth et al., 2020). The determination of the product costs allowed by the market and analysis of the current costs for the product functions and components reveal cost reduction needs and promote awareness in the company to constantly look for innovative solutions for cost reduction.

At the **process level**, for example, technology-oriented approaches, business process analyses, and the benchmarking concept can be used to identify problem areas and situations that require alternative and innovative solutions. Both the nature and quality of the processes (for example, degree of automation, errors, and duplicate work) and the process times and costs can be used to identify needs for innovation. The **Activity-based Costing approach** is particularly suitable for identifying cost reductions potentials (Friedl et al., 2022), as it can uncover overhead-intensive processes and thus help identify areas of action for innovative solutions (e.g., digitization, automation, and outsourcing of business processes).

In the area of **resources**, innovations are often necessary due to availability and cost reasons, as well as organizational, technical, and personnel developments. For determining innovation needs in resource provision, supplier relationships and contract designs can be examined, degrees of digitization and knowledge potentials can be checked, and make-or-buy analyses can be conducted. From a cost perspective, utilization, capacity, and cost structure analyses, as well as the **Total Cost of Ownership concept** can be used (Fischer et al., 2015) to identify specific problem situations for innovative cost reduction solutions.

Based on the results of the market and company-related investigation, specific problem-solving needs must now be derived, **innovation clusters** delineated, and clear **fields and goals of innovation** defined.

Tip
In this context, companies should pay particular attention to **describing the fields of innovation and the objectives pursued as clearly as possible**, in order to adequately determine the search space for innovative ideas and the costs of innovation. Various methods are available for identifying innovative problem situations, which are presented in the following Chap. 2.

After determining the innovation needs, the **search for specific potentials** to solve the identified problem situations or to exploit the recognized opportunities begins. Initially, market-, technology-, and cost-related ideas must be generated and then evaluated in terms of attractiveness and risk. Moreover, idea profiles with rough **solution sketches** should be developed and aligned with existing innovation activities.

Tip
In the **evaluation of ideas**, uniform criteria (e.g., market potential, profitability, adaptability, risk, acceptance, resilience, etc.) should be used to ensure

a transparent assessment and selection of innovation candidates. Based on this, a **roadmap** with corresponding prioritization of innovation activities should be created.

Important! Once management has finally approved an innovation project, development work should begin promptly. In addition to a **professional project definition, planning, and execution**, it is important to accompany the project with change management and active communication. The latter is especially important for disruptive innovations, as the success of innovation often requires a correspondingly high **willingness to change** among employees. For product or service innovations, activities from prototype construction to piloting and testing to production and marketing must be coordinated. For successful management of innovation activities in the individual process phases, it is also necessary to establish a transparent and comprehensive **management control system** for innovation processes in the company (see Sect. 6.2).

Key Insights of the Chapter

- Among the prerequisites for innovative thinking and action primarily involve **the will and the acting**—that is, the inner attitude towards creative work. As an introduction, five **creativity rules** are presented, which are based on the experiences of successful inventors.
- A central role in recognizing and solving innovation-demanding situations is played by **resolving internal contradictions** in the systems under consideration. Merely optimizing processes and products usually does not lead to innovations.
- The process of creative work is schematically and vividly represented in the **Invention Triangle**. It also becomes clear that a few basic methods—similar to basic arithmetic in elementary mathematics—can form the methodological basis for developing inventions. The analogy method, the variation method, and the combination method and their interplay through communication are briefly introduced.
- As **impulse generators** for inventive work in companies, the users of the products and processes and the contact persons to these users are predominantly effective. This leads to conclusions for the work of corporate innovation management.
- The **interplay of business management and technical development** is also of central importance. The impetus for innovative changes often arises from economic insights and requirements. This interaction should

already be conveyed and trained in professional education. Therefore, the methods of invention and their application should be integrated into the **teaching of business management** and likewise, in **technical education**, the economic requirements and effects, as well as the ecological and humanitarian aspects, should be comprehensively considered.

References

Baum, H.-G., Coenenberg, A., & Günther, T. (2013). *Strategisches Controlling*. Schäffer-Poeschel.

Brainyquote.com. (2021). www.brainyquote.com/quotes/thomas_a_edison_132683.

Brooks, S. S. (2017). Regulation and device development: Tips for optimizing your experience with the food and drug administration. *Techniques in Vascular & Interventional Radiology, 20*(2), 109–115. https://doi.org/10.1053/j.tvir.2017.04.001.

Busch, E. (2021). *Dissertation "Optimierung des Innovations- und Entwicklungsprozesses von bio medizintechnischen Geräten"*.

Busch, E., Roth, D., & Williams, J. (2009). *Blocking Publication " Vorrichtung zur Lagerung von Patienten auf Untersuchungs- und Op-Tischen"*. http://www.priorartregister.com/publikationen/suchergebnis/?tt_products%5Bsword%5D=System%20zur%20Bolussteuerung&cHash=0ccb15a99cfc1ebbe55c227851943a1e.

Busch, E., Bulitta, C., Nobach, K., & Strobel, N. (2021). Innovation & Entwicklung im globalen. *MED engineering, 4*, 56–58. https://med-eng.de/2021/10/28/innovation/.

Busch, E., Strobel, N., Nobach, K., Bulitta, C., Hirshfeld, J., Wu, L., & de Abreu, M. (2021b). Optimizing the innovation and development process of medical devices – A study based on angiographic equipment. *Health and Technology, 11*(3), 563–574. https://doi.org/10.1007/s12553-021-00537-7.

Busch, H. (1976). *Die Geburt erfinderischer Ideen*. Liesma.

Busch, K. H., & Busch, H. (1980). *Ideensuchverfahren im technischen Entwicklungsprozess*.

Cascio, J. (2020). Facing the Age of Chaos. https://medium.com/@cascio/facing-the-age-of-chaos-b00687b1f51d.

Conrad, W. (1980). *Wer-Was-Wann: Entdeckungen und Erfindungen in Naturwissenschaft und Technik*. Fachbuchverlag.

Fibitz, A. (2019). *Wertschöpfung durch Geschäftsmodellinnovationen: Festschrift für Prof. Dr. Ha bil. Wolfgang Becker zum 65. Geburtstag* (S. 671–702). Springer Gabler. https://doi.org/10.1007/978-3-658-18573-2_30.

Fischer, T., Möller, K., & Schultze, W. (2015). *Controlling: Grundlagen, Instrumente und Entwicklungsperspektiven*. Schäffer-Poeschel.

Friedl, G., Hofmann, C., & Pedell, B. (2022). *Kostenrechnung: Eine entscheidungsorientierte Einführung*. Vahlen. https://doi.org/10.15358/9783800668151.

Gemünden, H. G., & Littkemann, J. (2007). Innovationsmanagement und -controlling – Theoretische Grundlagen und praktische Implikationen. *Controlling & Management, 51*(3), 4–18. https://doi.org/10.1365/s12176-012-0171-6.

Granig, P. (2007). Innovationsbewertung Potentialprognose und -steuerung durch Ertrags- und Risikosimulation. *Gabler*. https://doi.org/10.1007/978-3-8350-5412-7.

Grupp, H. (1997). *Messung und Erklärung des Technischen Wandels: Grundzüge einer empirischen Innovationsökonomik*. Springer.

Horváth, P., Gleich, R., & Seiter, M. (2020). *Controlling* (14. Aufl.). Vahlen. https://www.vahlen.de/horvath-gleich-seiter-controlling/product/25337903.

Innovationsökonomik. (2022). Studysmarter.de. https://www.studysmarter.de/studium/bwl/mikrooekonomie-studium/innovationsoekonomik/.

Kaschny, M., Nolden, M., & Schreuder, S. (2015). *Innovationsmanagement im Mittelstand – Strategien, Implementierung, Praxisbeispiele* (1. Aufl.). Springer Gabler. https://doi.org/10.1007/978-3-658-02545-8.

Klaus, G., & Buhr, M. (1976). *Philosophisches Wörterbuch*. Bibliographisches Institut.

König, W. (1997). *Propyläen Technikgeschichte* (Bd. 4, S. 328). Ulstein Buchverlage GmbH.

Landwehr-Zloch, S. (2022). *Management und Controlling von Innovationen: Wertorientierung im Kontext von Bewertungsunsicherheit und Komplexität* (S. 1–21). https://doi.org/10.1007/978-3-658-04795-5_75-2.

Lee, J. (2014). *Average Cost of Angiography System Up 26% in June*. https://www.modernhealthcare.com/article/20141008/NEWS/310089965/average-cost-of-angiography-system-up-26-in-june.

Linde, H. (1988). *Gesetzmäßigkeiten, methodische Mittel und Strategien zur Bestimmung von Ent wicklungsaufgaben mit erfinderischer Zielstellung*.

Lohmann, H. (1960). *Zur Theorie und Praxis der Heuristik in der Ingenieurerziehung*.

Luther, M. (1950). Der kleine Katechismus Martin Luthers (S. 5–8). Evangelische Verlagsanstalt GmbH.

McDonald, M., & Brown, L. (1994). *Competitive Marketing Strategy for Europe* (1. Aufl., S. 1). Bloomsbury Publishing PLC.

Meyer, J. U. (2016). *Radikale Innovation: Das Handbuch für Marktrevolutionäre* (2. Aufl.). BusinessVillage.

Michel, U. (2017). Digitalisierung der Unternehmenssteuerung: Prozessautomatisierung, Business Analytics, Big Data, SAP S/4HANA, Anwendungsbeispiele. In *Controlling Digital Business Models* (S. 33–49). Schäffer-Poeschel.

Möhrle, M., & Specht, D. (2018). *Stichwort: Innovation*. Gabler Business Dictionary. https://wirtschaftslexikon.gabler.de/definition/innovation-39624/version-263028.

Möller, K., Schultze, W., & Steinmann, J.-C. (2016). Innovationscontrolling. In C. P. Hoffmann, S. Lennerts, C. Schmitz, W. Stölzle, & F. Uebernickel (Hrsg.), *Business Innovation: Das St. Galler Modell* (S. 141–162). Springer Fachmedien Wiesbaden. https://doi.org/10.1007/978-3-658-07167-7_10

Nelke, A. (2016). *Kommunikation und Nachhaltigkeit im Innovationsmanagement von Unternehmen* (1. Aufl.). Springer Gabler. https://doi.org/10.1007/978-3-658-14580-4.

Nobach, K. (2019). Bedeutung der Digitalisierung für das Controlling und den Controller. In P. Ulrich & B. Baltzer (Hrsg.), *Wertschöpfung in der Betriebswirtschaftslehre: Festschrift für Prof. Dr. Habil. Wolfgang Becker zum 65. Geburtstag* (S. 247–269). Springer Fachmedien Wiesbaden. https://doi.org/10.1007/978-3-658-18573-2_11.

Rusch, M., Treusch, O., David, U., & Seiter, M. (2016). Industrie 4.0–Controllers Aufgaben. *Controller Magazine, 3*, 70–79.

Ryckx, N., Sans-Merce, M., Meuli, R., Zerlauth, J., & Verdun, F. (2016). System upgrade on Philips Allura FD20 angiography systems: Effects on patient skin dose and static image quality. *Radiation Protection Dosimetry, 169*(1–4), 313–318. https://doi.org/10.1093/rpd/ncv484.

Schallmo, D., & Brecht, L. (2017). *Prozessinnovation erfolgreich anwenden: Grundlagen und me thodisches Vorgehen: Ein Management- und Lehrbuch mit Aufgaben und Fragen* (1. Aufl.). Springer Gabler. https://doi.org/10.1007/978-3-662-54504-1.

Schäperkötter, H. (2022). *Grundlagen des Innovationsmanagements: Orientierung und Anregungen für Praktiker* (1. Aufl.). Springer Gabler. https://doi.org/10.1007/978-3-658-37725-0.

Schuh, G., & Bender, D. (2012). Grundlagen des Innovationsmanagements. In G. Schuh (Hrsg.), *Innovation Management: Handbook of Production and Management 3* (2. Aufl., S. 1–16). Springer Vieweg. https://doi.org/10.1007/978-3-642-25050-7.

Schumpeter, J. (1961). *Konjunkturzyklen: Eine theoretische historische und statistische Analyse des kapitalistischen Prozesses*. Vandenhoeck & Ruprecht.

Sferrella, S. (2019). Equipment Service: Total Cost of Ownership. https://www.radiologybusiness.com/topics/technology-management/equipment-service-total-cost-ownership.

Siemens Healthineers. (2024, April). Options and Upgrades. https://www.siemens-healthineers.com/medical-imaging/medical-imaging-options-upgrades.

Stifterverband. (Hrsg.). (2022). Forschung und Entwicklung in der Wirtschaft 2020. https://www.stifterverband.org/fue-facts-2020.

Vahs, D., & Burmester, R. (2005). *Innovationsmanagement: Von der Produktidee zur erfolgreichen Vermarktung*. Schäffer-Poeschel.

Weis, B. X. (2022). *Praxishandbuch Innovation Leitfaden für Erfinder, Entscheider und Unterneh men* (1. Aufl.). Gabler. https://link.springer.com/book/10.1007/978-3-8349-3778-0#bibliographic-information

2 Efficient Methods for Identifying Innovative Problems

Abstract For a company's position in regional, national, and international competition, it is crucial to anticipate development trends and the resulting or changing problems in order to prepare for expected situations. However, this forward-looking orientation is not only indispensable for companies, but also for research institutes, educational institutions, ministries, disaster management, and national defense. The methods described in this chapter examine the situations and processes of interest from various perspectives, thus enabling specific insights. Predominantly intuitively oriented methods require relatively little effort and provide quick statements. This includes, for example, destructive brainstorming. The Delphi technique and scenario technique use expert statements, but proceed with more reliable statements in multi-level decision spaces. The portfolio technique bases its statements primarily on economic considerations, while the envelope curve theory essentially relies on technical parameters. The relationships in systems and processes are particularly taken into account in system analysis, technology impact assessment, process analysis, and product line analysis. In their practical application, combinations of several methods are possible and sensible, depending on the expected scope of the statements.

2.1 Selection and Application of Suitable Methods

Tools for identifying innovative problems and developing action strategies are

- Evaluation of research results
- Forecasting methods, trend analysis, envelope curve theory
- System analysis, function analysis, process analysis
- Technology impact assessment
- Value analysis
- Weakness analysis

E. Busch et al., *Methodology of Innovation*, Contributions to Management Science,
https://doi.org/10.1007/978-3-658-50010-8_2

- Checklists
- Destructive brainstorming
- Delphi Technique
- Scenario Technique
- Portfolio Technique

2.2 System Analysis

Example from Medical Engineering "New low-radiation technology increases radiation dose"
After nine years of development, St. Jude Medical's MediGuide Technology brought a new 3D navigation system to the market. The marketing promise was to reduce the need for fluoroscopy during the examination and thus the X-ray dose. (Abbott, 2016; todaysmedicaldevelopments.com, 2012)

MediGuide is a technology that overlays catheter information on existing, patient-specific imaging material using augmented reality. This imaging material is usually generated at the beginning of the procedure, possibly controlled by breathing and EKG, and then overlaid with a symbolic representation of the catheter (see Fig. 2.1). (Desert Regional Medical Center, 2013)

The industry partner reported in the context of the joint integration project that a renowned cardiologist had formulated his experiences with the use of a new technology at a European congress: "The use of MediGuide technology leads to higher X-ray dose exposures in electrophysiological examinations than without this technology."

The verification of this statement confirmed the user's experience.

It turned out that a dose program was defined as standard in an early development step, which led to this result.

In a **first iteration**, recommendations for the usable dose programs were created and the corresponding systems were configured by the application specialists.

This required a high amount of travel and work for these specialists, which grows with an increasing number of installed systems.

This resulted in the motivation for optimization in a **second iteration loop**.

In cooperation with the German Heart Center in Munich, the requirements regarding acceptable image quality and radiation dose were defined.

In dialogue with the users, the engineers iteratively optimized the system parameters until the best result according to the ALARA principle was achieved.

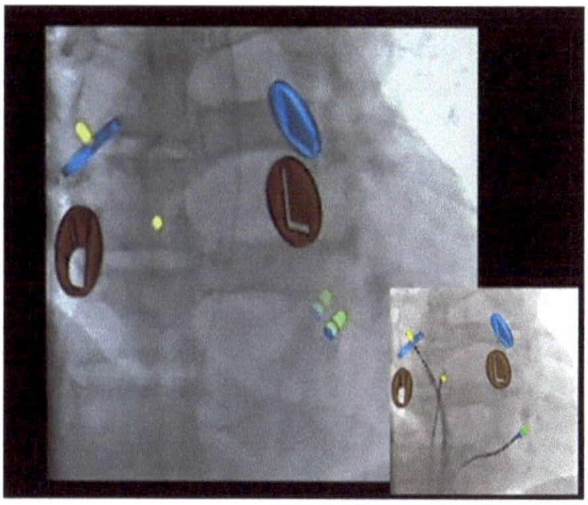

Fig. 2.1 MediGuide Technology—Use of symbolic overlay on EKG and breath-synchronized X-ray series

These settings were verified in a study. The result, a reduction of the radiation dose by 77%, was published by the users in the journal "EP Europace". (Bourier et al., 2016)

After clinical evaluation, these dose programs are standard in the delivered angiography systems. ◀

Example from Medical Engineering "Downtime of medical devices due to maintenance"

The trend in medical diagnostics and therapy is towards specialized facilities with several laboratories for the same modality. The invention described below refers to the described environment (see Fig. 2.2).

The problem statement referred to disruptions of clinical operations due to downtime caused by maintenance.

In the analysis of the problem statement, doctors, technical department at healthcare providers, users of imaging systems, and colleagues were involved.

The short text of the invention report (E. Busch, 2003) "Modular computer structure in left heart catheter laboratories" states: "The contradictions are characterized by the fact that

1. *so far, for each system separately, a fixed, system-bound allocation of licenses for recording modes (e.g., Digital Subtraction Angiography) or post-processing software (quantification of stenoses) has been made—but never all software packages in can be used in all laboratories simultaneously,*
2. *each system is addressed separately for maintenance and software upgrade/update by installing software updates* viadata *carriers (e.g., CD)—but the upgrade involves considerable time and personnel effort,*
3. *"customized", dedicated solutions for all functional units, including IT components, were developed in-house—but compared to the IT industry,*

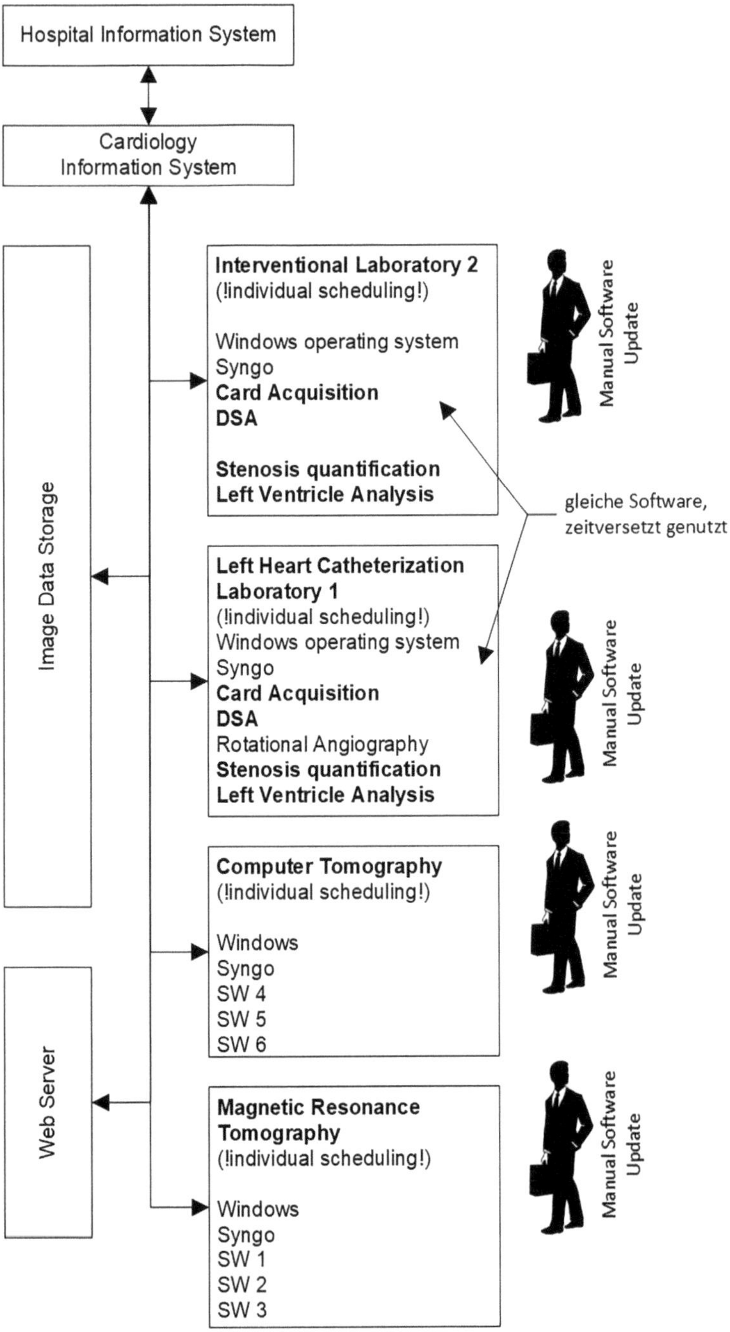

Fig. 2.2 IT Infrastructure of Interventional Laboratories. (Adapted from Busch, 2003)

only small batch sizes were produced and longer times passed until market launch, and

4. *integration into existing IT networks is desired and contemporary—but the corresponding security concepts for protection against viruses and information theft of personal medical data are lacking.*
5. *For effective utilization, the examinations in the LI-IK must be planned—but for central optimization of daily planning, the information in the individual LHK and in the hospital information system is missing or must be handled manually."*

From this, the task was derived to find a solution that minimizes disruptions to clinical operations.

Using the analogy method and optimization as working methods, the following solution approach was described in the short text of the invention report (E. Busch, 2003) "Modular computer structure in left heart catheter laboratories":

"The system architecture outlined in

Figure 2.3 is used.

The client in the control room has a configurable workstation that includes image information, case reports, export of image information (e.g., on print media). The hardware requirements are minimized. The image data is temporarily stored on the client and securely archived on the server in parallel.

1. *The server temporarily assigns application licenses to the clients. On this basis, new billing models such as "floating licenses" or "pay per use" can be realized for interventional labs.*
2. *The software updates are sent to the server once and then automatically duplicated from the server to the clients.*
3. *Standard IT solutions are used for the clients and servers, which available off the shelf.*
4. *Firewall and virus scanner are installed on the server, protecting the downstream network of clients from viruses and the information theft of personal medical data.*
5. *Based on the "worklist" available on the server for the day, the procedures are distributed to the individual interventional labs in such a way that optimal utilization is achieved."* ◄

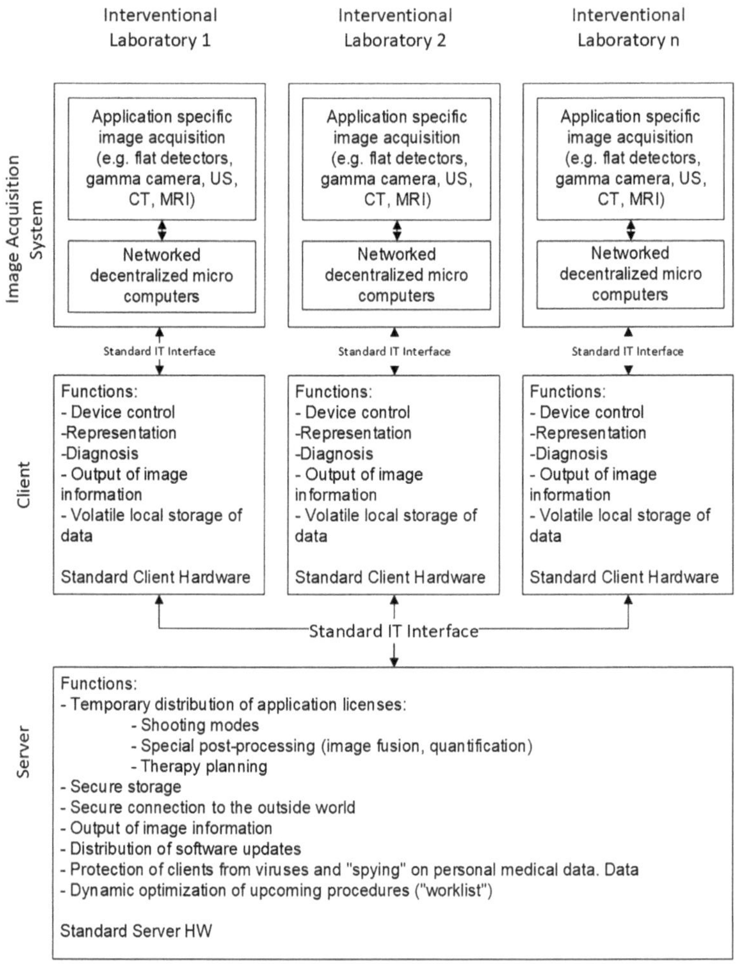

Fig. 2.3 Modular computer structure. (Adapted from Busch, 2003)

2.3 The Portfolio Technique

Portfolios are used in many areas with different objectives and approaches. After the portfolio technique was developed in the financial industry around 1952 to achieve an optimal investment with the lowest possible risk and maximum success, this method is now widely used. In this section, we focus on the product portfolio. The goal is to identify promising business areas and define innovation and leadership strategies.

When developing a product portfolio, the objects (products, processes, brands) of the target field (business field) must be assessed or objectively evaluated in terms of

- their relative market share and
- market growth

to be estimated or objectively evaluated.

This evaluation allows the objects to be classified into the fields of a matrix. (Fleig, 2022)

A commonly used four-field table includes the groups

- Question Marks,
- Star,
- Cash Cow, and
- Poor Dogs.

Working with the portfolio matrix and especially the insights and results obtained are usually treated as strictly confidential—as fundamental management tools. However, in many cases, insightful knowledge can be gained from publicly accessible media.

In the following example of Siemens Healthineers, the portfolio matrix is derived from the mentioned publicly available press releases.

- Siemens acquires Corindus (Höpner & Teigheder, 2019)
- Siemens acquires Varian (Müller & Deckstein, 2020)
- Medical IT Solutions sold to Cerner (*Cerner's Siemens Acquisition: What Does It Mean?*, 2014; Wonneberger, 2014)
- Patient monitors sold to Dräger (Siemens, 2009)
- Expansion of Forchheim site (*Siemens Healthineers expands Forchheim site*, 2021)
- Siemens Healthineers IPO (Schneid, 2017)

In the matrix, in addition to the general explanation of the matrix field, the relevant products or business areas are classified (see Fig. 2.4).

The individual products or business areas will be briefly explained below for better understanding.

Background, Additional Information

Robots for vascular surgical procedures (Question Mark)

Robot-assisted vascular surgical procedures are becoming increasingly important.

> "For example, if a stent needs to be placed in a thrombosis, the doctor can do this from the next room using a joystick. The procedure is thus more precise and faster. The doctor is also exposed to less radiation." (Höpner & Teigheder, 2019)

This business area is not without risk. Further research and subsequent innovations are required. The business area needs to be made profitable.

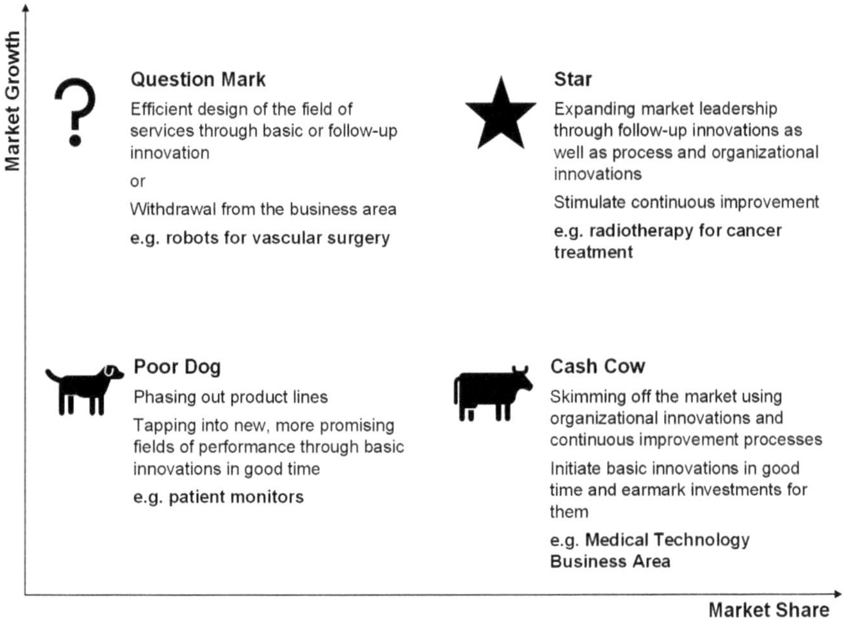

Fig. 2.4 Portfolio Matrix

Background, Additional Information:
Cancer Radiation Therapy (Star)
"Instead, the company's CEO and his board colleagues are tying their acquisition to something familiar and proven: their imaging devices such as computer or magnetic resonance tomographs (CTs and MRIs).

Because the latest acquisition target, Varian, is considered one of the world leaders in radiation systems used in cancer treatment. Radiation is one of the solid pillars in the treatment of cancer—especially planning using software is more precise than ever before.

As a result, it has gained in importance recently, especially in combination with other treatment strategies such as chemotherapy or surgery. Siemens Healthineers could link its CTs and MRIs more closely with Varian's devices, especially in the area of software. Data about the exact location of the tumor, but also its drainage areas, could then be transferred directly to the radiation software. This would probably be touted as a selling point for large devices from Siemens to hospitals.

If the deal goes through as planned, other medical engineering companies would miss out, especially Siemens' main competitors Philips (Netherlands) and GE Healthcare (USA). It is assumed in the industry that the battle for the Swedish company Elekta will then begin. It shares a large part of the market for radiation medicine with Varian. Siemens has spoiled the prices with the absurd valuation for Varian—a takeover "Elekta would therefore likely also be correspondingly high-priced."

(Müller & Deckstein, 2020)

"Siemens Turns Cash Cow Medical Engineering into a Stock Market Star"

And so Kaeser, whose contract has just been extended until 2021, is planning his next coup: Medical technology, a cash cow of the company for some time, is going public through the sale of new shares in 2018.

However, the entire Siemens Group performed weaker than expected by industry experts in the third business quarter. This was also due to significantly fewer orders compared to the same period last year. Significant declines had to be taken by the newly formed wind business Siemens Gamesa and the power generation division Power and Gas. On Thursday, however, it was announced that Siemens, as part of a consortium, secured a major contract for a wind power project in Turkey.

In the Power and Gas division, where the turbine business is bundled, order intake fell by 41% and revenues fell by twelve percent. The business suffers from overcapacity and price pressure. Higher restructuring costs additionally depressed the result, which decreased by 23%. Restructuring costs also burdened Siemens Gamesa's wind energy business." (Schneid, 2017)

Background, Additional Information:
Patient Monitors (Poor Dogs)
"Siemens will sell its 25% stake in Dräger Medical AG & Co. KG to majority owner Dräger. The medical engineering company will then be fully owned by Dräger. The sales proceeds amount to at least around 250 million euros. The board of Drägerwerk Verwaltungs AG as personally liable partner of Drägerwerk AG & Co. KGaA and the board of Siemens AG have agreed on this. The execution of the transaction is still subject to the approval of the antitrust authorities.

Siemens and Dräger have decided on this step to reduce complexity on both sides. "Wherever it is beneficial for our customers, we will continue and expand the good cooperation of our companies in the future. This applies in particular to technological solutions at the interface between diagnostics and therapy," said Hermann Requardt, CEO of the Siemens Healthcare sector. In 2003, Siemens had brought the business of the electromedicine division into Dräger's medical engineering business and had participated with a 35% stake in Dräger Medical AG & Co. KGaA. In 2007, Siemens reduced its stake to 25%." (Siemens, 2009)

2.4 The Envelope Curve Technique

The development of performance parameters of biological, technical, or organizational systems generally follows an S-shaped course, a growth curve (see Fig. 2.5).

After a (usually difficult) start phase (at t_{E1}), a progressive growth phase begins, which after passing a turning point at time t_{W1} transitions into a regressive phase and comes close to stagnation from time t_{S1}.

At a time t_{E2}, the conditions for qualitative further development (quality leap) through an innovative solution are created. The quantitative development of the original system continues for a while. The old and new system coexist during this time.

The timing for initiating a new development depends on the type of systems considered. In conventional technical systems, new development usually begins when about 85% of the development potential has been exhausted. In high technologies (e.g., in circuit development), new solutions appear when only about 33% of the possible performance has been achieved. The time t_{E2} therefore lies within a relatively wide tolerance field.

The envelope curve shown in Fig. 2.5 results from the alternation of quantitative and qualitative developments in the subject area under consideration.

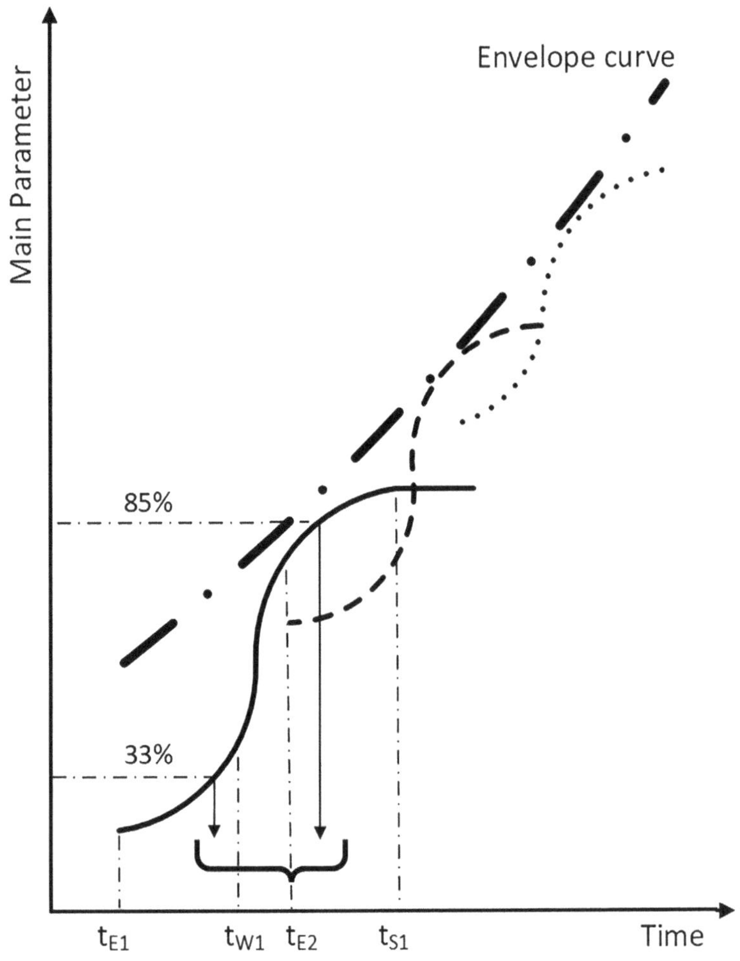

Fig. 2.5 Development curves

Example
A representative example of development curves in medical engineering is the **transition from image intensifiers to flat detectors in angiography.** This started in the year 2000.
The underlying principle is different for **Image Intensifiers (II)** and **Flat Panel Detectors (FPD)**. This resulted in theoretical technical advantages for the Flat Panel Detectors. For example, aging was no longer a relevant issue with the FPD.
However, the new manufacturing processes for the FPD were more expensive during the ramp-up phase and had higher failure rates. This was a factor that led to the market prices for FPD being a multiple of II.

This was established and compensated for as a competitive advantage through appropriate marketing strategies by hospital operators, especially in the USA.

Initially, for the clinical user, there were no clinical advantages when considering the technology of II and FPD separately, as the image quality and the resulting dose were comparable for both technologies.

This changed in later iterations in favor of the FPD.

(Chase et al., 2015; Kottou et al., 2004)

In 2003, it was communicated to hospital operators that

- the flat panel detector technology has a higher potential for future developments in terms of improved contrast resolution.
- the flat panel detector technology as the next generation digital solution will replace the image intensifier/TV chain in the future.
- both alternatives will be offered to the customer for a transition period. ◄

2.5 The Delphi Technique

The name of this method refers to the Oracle of Delphi. The prophetess and priestess Pythia sat on a tripod and provided the seekers of advice in the Apollo temple with ambiguous sayings vague predictions for expected events or gave instructions for future plans. (Schwab, 1959)

Thus, Heracles received the oracle's prophecy that he must serve three years of servitude to be freed from his affliction—which the gods had imposed on him as punishment for the murder of Iphitos. After these three years, he set out to perform some of his known heroic deeds.

The posthumous honorable burial of Theseus was also ordered by the Oracle of Delphi, after his spirit led the Greeks to victory against a tenfold superior force of Persians.

With higher prediction certainty, the Federal Ministry of Education and Research has been publishing the results of expert surveys as Delphi reports since 1993. Examples include "German Delphi Report on the Development of Science and Technology" and "Potentials and Dimensions of the Knowledge Society—Impacts on Educational Processes and Educational Structures" (Stock, 1998).

These extensive materials contain predictions for the development in important fields.

The principle of the Delphi technique is that experienced experts are surveyed anonymously in several rounds. After each survey round, the statements are condensed and fed back to the experts. In the subsequent round, the found results are to be further specified. With this approach, three to four cycles are possible and meaningful.

The following questions are intended to illustrate this procedure:

First Cycle	What methods of cancer early detection and cancer disease can be expected in the future?
Feedback	List of diagnostic and therapeutic methods
Second Cycle	Cycle: Can the compiled list be expanded? How is the importance of the listed methods to be assessed?
Feedback	Completed list Ranking
Third Cycle	In which development phase are the listed methods? What inhibiting factors can occur for each individual method? How is the demand for each method to be assessed? In what timeframe can the method be realized?
Feedback	Table with quantitative expert assessments

The results can form the basis for expert meetings and workshops to build a consensus of opinions. They need to be further refined by experts and prepared for decision-making processes.

Example

Advisory councils are often well established in the strategy or portfolio process in practice. (Siemens, 2021)

The success of these events largely depends on the individuals, the conditions, and the methodology.

The **selection of individuals** who are invited as advisors should be made considering the goals to be achieved. In which market segment are they active? Are they successful and well-known personalities at the end of their careers or young talents with a lot of potential? Are they primarily networkers or opinion leaders or experts?

Psychology may play an important role in the **selection of conditions**. Do you choose the venue as realistically as possible, e.g., in a typical work environment, or visionary at an inspiring place, e.g., in an observatory, in rooms with a view over a wide landscape.

The **methodology of leadership** of the advisors through the design of the event program and the selection of topics requires a lot of care. A mix of initial presentation of the advisors on trends and focused evaluation of new developments by the advisors has proven successful. This approach ensures that the market segment is considered holistically at the beginning and thus previously unconsidered topics are identified and then previously identified detailed topics are discussed.

For the **collection of feedback** from the advisors, an open question format is recommended, as it allows more degrees of freedom in the response than closed ones. This may bring potentially new solution variants into the conversation.

For example: "What are the 5 problems that bother you the most every day?" or "What are the 5 things you would improve about the current technology?"

A **recursive reality check** helps to verify the relevance of the problem/ potential solution. This can be achieved by asking the following questions: "What would change for you if the problem were solved?" or "What impact would this have on the quality of your work results, your workflow, and the financial result of your business?".

It is advisable to ask which **external conditions might support or hinder this solution approach**?

Finally, the **evaluation of the topics** from the initial presentation of the advisors and the presented developments should take place, e.g., by weighting according to the (cost-)benefit ratio.

The **regular communication with the participants** of the advisory council about the progress is recommended in order to continuously provide feedback for the innovation and development process or to support marketing and distribution activities with the help of the networkers and opinion leaders. ◀

2.6 The Scenario Technique

The name of this approach is borrowed from the theater environment. The stage design and the scenery in the theater form the thematic framework for the action, for the scenes.

The scenario technique involves thinking ahead to various possibilities (scenarios) for future situations and working out alternative paths (paths) into future spaces, see Fig. 2.6.

The procedure can be divided into the following eight steps:

- Clarification of the problem
- Specification of the statement goal
- Description of the initial situation
- Obtaining the necessary information
- Determination of time horizons
- Identification of influencing factors
- Recording of influencing factors (e.g., with card circulation technique or brainstorming)
- Bundling (clustering) of factors (forming superordinate terms)
- Determining Development Directions (Trends)
- Developing Variants/Alternatives

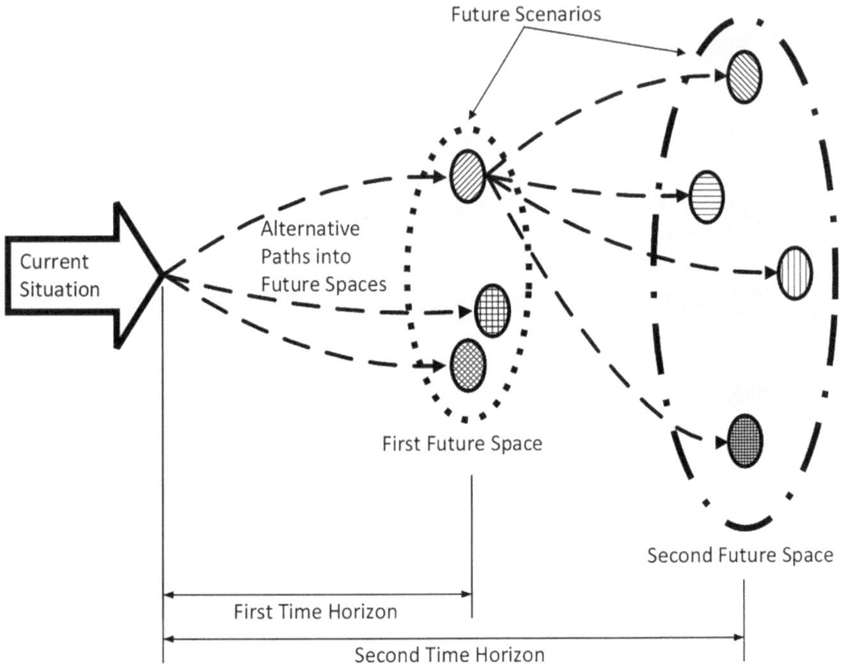

Fig. 2.6 Scenario Technique

- Illustrating the Interrelationships of Effects
- Identifying Interactions (Interdependencies) between Influencing Factors
- Developing a System Analysis (Structure of the Interrelationships of Effects)
- Anticipating Disruptive Events
- Anticipating Possible Disruptive Events (e.g., through Brainstorming or Delphi Method)
- Developing Scenarios for the Chosen Time Horizons
- Deriving Consequences
- Developing Strategies

Every solved problem, every developed solution is a source and starting point for new problem statements. Wilhelm Busch succinctly and memorably put it this way: *"Every wish, once fulfilled, instantly breeds offspring."* (Busch, 1909, p. 365)

After solving a problem, it is therefore necessary to check,

- how the rsulting solution can be transferred to other cases and areas (means-purpose relationship) and
- how newly arisen subsequent problems can be specified and addressed.

2.7 The Process Analysis

Example

A practical example: In 2015, one of the authors was commissioned to achieve a **turnaround in a problem situation** where the order intake for product family A had been stagnating within a narrow range for years.

After a **thorough analysis of the market situation and our own marketing mix**—consisting of marketing, product, price, and sales—the greatest potential for improvement was identified in sales.

For a **cause determination, a dialogue was conducted with sales colleagues worldwide**. It became apparent that sales of product A were stagnating because sales were primarily focused on other product families.

In response to the **question of why**, a valuable problem hint from sales for the cause of the low sales of product A: "*For the configuration of product A, I need just as much time as for product B with ten times the sales price. Where do you think I invest my time if the commission is proportional to the sales price?*"

In the following dialogue, the cause at the next level of detail became visible. A complex price book required significant effort and a high level of detailed knowledge to create a correct offer for product A.

This led to the approach of simplifying the price book for product A. The goal of this measure was accordingly formulated that the effort and commission are in a ratio accepted by sales and comparable with other product families.

As a test, this approach was presented and confirmed in dialogue with sales as a solution to the identified problem—stagnating order intake.

This was followed by an analysis of demand and purchasing behavior, the corresponding packaging of available options, and ultimately the determination of content and price positioning.

The **achieved solution** is characterized by a significant reduction in the complexity of the web-based price book and thus the decisions to be made and the required knowledge.

Through the **process analysis**, the **specification of the task**, and the **optimization of the visible system structure**, an initial growth of 40% could be achieved within two years.

As a side effect, an **increased perceived competence of the provider** by the customer and thus an **increased attractiveness of the overall portfolio** for the customer was observed.

The estimated process duration was 30 weeks.

In a **second iteration**, additional software-based support was provided to sales for this product. Using "guided selling" the time required to create a proposal was further reduced by 73% based on customer-friendly questions.

The order intake of product A increased by 100% over a period of seven years. ◀

2.8 The Product Line Analysis

The product line analysis allows us to estimate the ecological, economic, and societal effects a product generates (Klöpffer, 1991). The sum of the effects of the entire product portfolio is then made visible, as seen in the Sustainability Report, 2021 of Siemens on page 16 (*Sustainability* Report, 2021, 2021, p. 16).

Key Insights of the Chapter

- Recognizing and realizing innovation-demanding situations should not be left to chance in companies.
- The **innovation strategies** must ensure that companies adapt in a timely and forward-looking manner to expected market situations, scientific findings, and economic policy trends.
- The **innovation management** has several tools available to identify innovation-demanding situations. The system and process analysis, portfolio technique, envelope technique, Delphi technique, and scenario technique are particularly illustrated with examples.
- These approaches are complemented by insights from operational controlling.

References

Abbott. (2016). *Navigating away from live X-ray*. https://www.cardiovascular.abbott/content/dam/bss/divisionalsites/cv/pdf/guides/15345_SJM-MDG-0814-0002(1)_clinicalCompendium_r4_(Final).pdf. Accessed 15. Sept. 2024.

Bourier, F., Reents, T., Ammar-Busch, S., Buiatti, A., Kottmaier, M., Semmler, V., Telishevska, M., Brkic, A., Grebmer, C., Lennerz, C., Kolb, C., Hessling, G., & Deisenhofer, I. (2016). Evaluation of a new very low dose imaging protocol: Feasibility and impact on X-ray dose levels in electrophysiology procedures. *EP Europace, 18*(9), 1406–1410. https://doi.org/10.1093/europace/euv364

Busch, E. (2003). *Interne Erfindungsmeldung „Modulare Rechnerstruktur bei Linksherzkatheterla boren (LHK)"*.

Busch, W. (1909). Niemals. In Schein und Sein (p. 365). Lothar Joachim. http://www.zeno.org/nid/20004610008. Accessed 15. Sept. 2024.

Cerner's Siemens Acquisition: What Does It Mean? (2014). https://www.ecgmc.com/thought-leadership/blog/cerners-siemens-acquisition-what-does-it-mean. Accessed 15. Sept. 2024.

Chase, D., Varghese, A., George, P. V., George, O. K., & Livingstone, R. S. (2015). Transition from image intensifier to flat panel detector in interventional cardiology: Impact of radiation dose. *Journal of Medical Physics, 40*, 24. https://doi.org/10.4103/0971-6203.152241.

Desert Regional Medical Center (Director). (2013, August). *Catheter Ablation to Treat Atrial Fibrillation and Heart Rhythm Disorders*. https://www.youtube.com/watch?v=sktm9ZF733k. Accessed 15. Sept. 2024.

Fleig, J. (2022). *Portfoliotechnik und Portfolioanalyse*. https://www.business-wissen.de/hb/portfoliotechnik-und-portfolio-diagramme-fuer-die-strategieplanung-nutzen/. Accessed 15. Sept. 2024.

Höpner, A., & Teigheder, M. (2019). *Milliarden-Wette auf die Zukunft: Siemens Healthineers über nimmt US-Firma Corindus*. https://www.handelsblatt.com/unternehmen/industrie/medizintechnik-milliarden-wette-auf-die-zukunft-siemens-healthineers-uebernimmt-us-firma-corindus/24882598.html. Accessed 15. Sept. 2024.

Klöpffer, W. (1991). *Produktlinienanalyse und Ökobilanz—Methodische Ansätze zur rationalen Be urteilung von Produkten unter Umweltaspekten, 3,* 114–118.

Kottou, S., Kollaros, N., Dafnomili, P., Koutelou, M., Vano, E., Neofotistou, V., & Tsapaki, V. (2004). Comparison of a conventional and a flat-panel digital system in interventional cardiology procedures. *British Journal of Radiology, 77*, 562–567. https://doi.org/10.1259/bjr/83257582.

Müller, M., & Deckstein, D. (2020). *Siemens riskante Milliardenwette*. https://www.spiegel.de/wirtschaft/unternehmen/siemens-uebernahme-von-varian-die-gewagte-milliarden-wette-a-b6ff2ad6-e4f0-4bf3-8232-9e05cc82ef99. Accessed 15. Sept. 2024.

Schneid, H. (2017). *Siemens macht Cashcow Medizintechnik zum Börsestar*. https://www.diepresse.com/5262956/siemens-macht-cashcow-medizintechnik-zum-boersestar. Accessed 15. Sept. 2024.

Schwab, G. (1959). *Die schönsten Sagen des klassischen Altertums*. Altberliner.

Siemens. (Ed.). (2021). *Customer Advisory Council*. https://new.siemens.com/us/en/products/automation/process-analytics/customer-advisory-council.html. Accessed 15. Sept. 2024.

Siemens Healthineers baut Standort Forchheim aus. (2021). https://med-eng.de/2021/11/02/siemens-healthineers/. Accessed 15. Sept. 2024.

Siemens. (2009). *Press Release „Siemens verkauft seinen Anteil an der Dräger Medical AG & Co. KG an Dräger"*. https://press.siemens.com/global/de/pressemitteilung/siemens-verkauft-seinen-anteil-der-draeger-medical-ag-co-kg-draeger. Accessed 15. Sept. 2024.

Stock, J. (1998). Delphi – Bericht 1996/1998, Prognos AG, Basel, Publisher: Munich, Infratest Burke Social Research.

Sustainability Report 2021. (2021). https://corporate.webassets.siemens-healthineers.com/e585979ac3319b35/1ba3d260915b/Siemens-Healthineers_Sustainability-Report_2021.pdf. Accessed 15. Sept. 2024.

todaysmedicaldevelopments.com. (2012, October 9). *St. Jude Medical announces launch of its MediGuide technology*. Today's Medical Developments. https://www.todaysmedicaldevelopments.com/article/st-jude-mediguide-technology-100912/. Accessed 15. Sept. 2024.

Wonneberger, K. (2014). *Siemens will Krankenhaus-IT an Cerner verkaufen*. https://www.nordbayern.de/region/erlangen/siemens-will-krankenhaus-it-an-cerner-verkaufen-1.3815060. Accessed 15. Sept. 2024.

3
Diagnosis of the Problem Situation

Abstract The word "diagnosis" evokes associations that remind us of a doctor's visit, troubleshooting a car, or monitoring and maintaining large technical systems. All these situations have in common that through (dia) knowledge (gnosis), the foundations for further therapy, repair, or maintenance are created. Without a precise analysis, the further work on solving the problem often remains a tiring and unsatisfactory game of trial and error. To ensure that the diagnosis is targeted and effective, this chapter presents some proven approaches in the form of questionnaires and guidelines, explained with examples. It is essential—in the context of diagnosis—to get to the core of the identified problem and uncover contradictions in the system under consideration. Such contradictions—which both condition each other and exclude each other—can arise from conflicting desires, organizational conditions, or natural scientific laws.

3.1 System Analytical Perspective

With the recognition of a problem, there is a still vague statement that solving a problem could be meaningful or necessary. At this stage of recognition, there is generally not enough information available for the search for solution variants or even for the development of a design for a product, a process, or a new organizational solution.

The **diagnosis of the problem situation** starts from a recognized problem and leads to a refined problem statement through systematic preparation. The refined problem statement has several functions to fulfill.

1. First, it is the **basis** for the subsequent work steps;
2. therefore, it must contain all essential information for its rational processing.
3. Second, it is the most important source for **motivating** the workers;
4. it must stimulate, convince, and inspire.

E. Busch et al., *Methodology of Innovation*, Contributions to Management Science,
https://doi.org/10.1007/978-3-658-50010-8_3

5. Third, the refined problem statement is the **basis for contract design** or the agreements between the problem poser (as the client) and the worker (as the contractor);
6. it must precisely determine the goal and conditions in the mutual interest.

The editor, the team of editors, or the editing group must consider, among other things, the most accurate possible answers to the following questions:

- What specific purpose should the result serve and what needs should it satisfy?
- What contradictions need to be resolved?
- What result should be achieved?
- In what form should it be presented?
- What qualitative and quantitative metrics need to be achieved?
- When should the result or interim results be available?
- What is the cost of the development process?
- How is the economic viability of the solution ensured?
- What prerequisites need to be established for the editing process?
- What is already available and accessible?
- What prerequisites are necessary for a successful implementation of the result?
- What side effects could occur?
- Which of the side effects are desired and which are undesirable?
- Under what circumstances is the problem being addressed?

Therefore, in Fig. 3.1 a scheme for preparing problem statements for the development of technical solutions is presented, based on the approach in systematic heuristics (Koch, 1983).

This guideline fits into the following work steps:

- Critical examination of the appropriateness of the problem statement
- Precise definition of the goal
- Classification into the overarching system, definition of the overall function

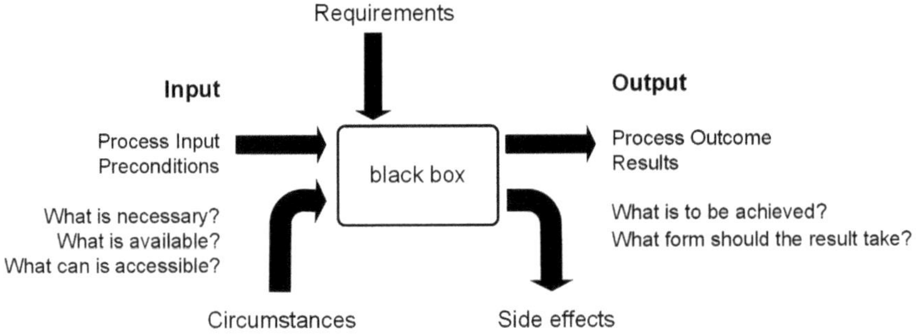

Fig. 3.1 Scheme for preparing problem statements

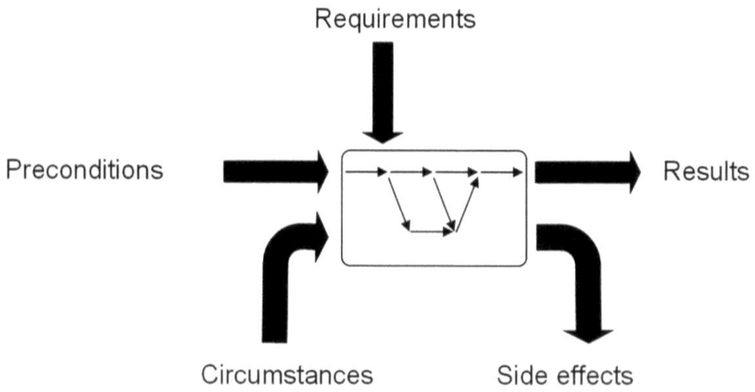

Fig. 3.2 Guideline for preparing problem statements for the development of technical solutions presented

- Precise definition of specifications and requirements
- Development of the current status
- Identification of subtasks
  - Recognize and organize sub-problems
  - Derive subtask statements and represent relations between them
- Planning of the solution path and resources

For application in individual disciplines, the scheme in Fig. 3.2 is often too general. Therefore, the following are guidelines for preparing problem statements for the development of technical solutions (Koch, 1983).

Prerequisites	Are there new scientific findings? Are there changes in customer behavior? Are changes (prices, delivery restrictions) to be expected from suppliers (materials, preliminary services)? What new technological processes are there? What changes can be expected from our own personnel? Are there changes in patent law?
Needs	What needs have been identified? What overarching objectives, strategies, or visions exist? What contradictions and trends have been identified? What are the starting points and weaknesses? What purpose should the result serve?

Results	What goal should be achieved? What new goals can be expected? What parameters should be achieved? Are changes in the standard or approval values to be expected? What new guidelines should be considered?
Circumstances	What resources are available (time, personnel, technical and financial resources, …)? What can be beneficial (regional and international collaborations)? What can hinder (patent situation, import regulations, delivery and performance times)?
Side Effects	Desired side effects (patents, licenses, publications, scientific generalizations) Side effects to avoid (losses, environmental impacts)

Data storage for targeted information gathering and project management programs can be used as tools for problem processing.

When formulating the goal (output), it quickly becomes apparent that the process in which the development result (the innovation) is to be used needs to be examined more closely. For this, a process analysis is useful. The overall process is broken down into its

- individual operations (elements) and
- the (logical, informational, material or energetic) connections (relations) between the operations

are broken down.

At the same time, the **operators** that cause the individual **operations** need to be identified. For this, the representation in Fig. 3.3 is useful.

The analysis of a process will be illustrated using an example.

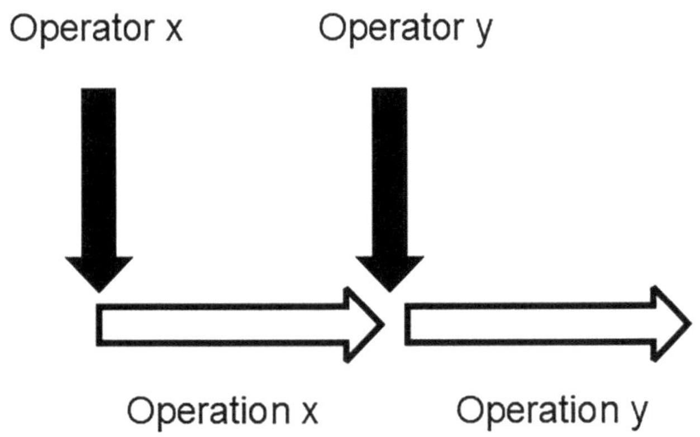

Fig. 3.3 Operators and operations in process analysis

Example

The development of a veterinary medical device system

The scientific, technical, and economic collaboration of engineers and scientists from Eastern European countries took place largely within the framework of projects in joint international working groups from 1949 to 1991.

The following example is intended to illustrate some aspects of this special innovation transfer.

The international trend towards large-scale animal husbandry requires a corresponding biotechnological organization of reproduction and optimal exploitation of the genetic potential of female breeding animals and male animals. With this goal in mind, a "Temporary International Research Collective Egg Transplantation" was established in 1973 under the leadership of the Research Center for The Animal Production Department of the Academy of Agricultural Sciences was formed. In this project, 25 scientists from seven Eastern European countries collaborated. A significant outcome of this collaboration was the development of non-surgical transfer procedures, replacing the previously common surgical embryo extraction. (Busch, 2009b)

Implementing such comprehensive scientific research results into technical solutions requires multidisciplinary and interdisciplinary collaboration across various fields, including precision engineering, which plays a crucial role.

The development of the device system for embryo transfer and its integration into the reproductive processes of farm animals had to follow the same rules as the development of system solutions or machine systems for other technical processes. From this perspective, the device system for embryo transfer was understood as a whole of various technical tools, coordinated and complementing each other in terms of their technical and technological parameters, for carrying out the entire embryo transfer procedure.

From this analysis, in interdisciplinary and multinational coordination, the following could be derived:

- The objective for designing the overall process,
- The foundations for the project management of the research and transfer project,
- The refined problem statement for a "fertilization biology device system"
- And the task definitions for the individual devices of the system.
- For the embryo transfer device system, in addition to the use of standard veterinary instruments, the development, testing, and manufacturing of the following devices were required:
- Device technology for examining uterine motility
- Ultrasound-guided follicle puncture devices
- Flushing devices for oocyte retrieval
- Computer-assisted image evaluation systems for locating and evaluating oocytes and embryos

- Devices for cultivating oocytes and embryos
- Containers for the mobile transport of biological materials
- Micromanipulators for biological objects
- Programmable deep-freezing facilities for embryos and somatic cell material
- Generators for the fusion of embryonic cells
- Implantation catheters

This example, illustrated in Fig. 3.4, shows the close link between the development of device technology for agricultural research and medical technology. This collaboration was mutually beneficial from the development of biotechnical procedures and device technical solutions. The close intertwining became even more apparent in the following development tasks (Busch, 2003):

- Device for immediate diagnosis of skull fractures (Patent DD 225 045 A1 from 04.07.1983)
- Device for closing blood vessels in the animal body (Patent DD 224 487 A1 from 12.06.1984)
- Method and device for castrating male farm animals (Patent DD 269 554 A1 from 29.12.1987)
- Pneumatic massage device (Patent DD 227 881 A1 from 02.10.1984)
- Device for driving artificial hearts (Patent DD 218 558 A1 from 20.04.1983)

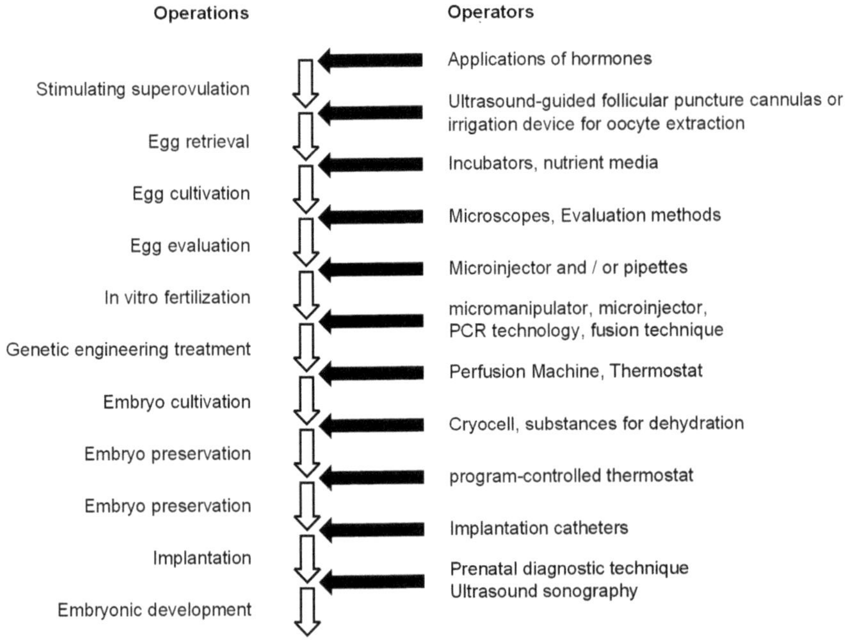

Fig. 3.4 Analysis of the "Embryo Transfer" system in a simplified representation

In addition to the development and international use of the methods and devices, important insights were gained in the field of fertilization biology and made available to the research institutions and companies of the participating countries.

Among the members of the international research group, a culture of communication and learning developed that could be carried forward into further projects and university teaching (see Fig. 3.5). The professional training and further education of veterinarians and veterinary medical technical assistants could be enriched with current insights. ◀

In another example, this analysis led to

- the goal setting for the design of the overall process,
- the basics for the project management of the research and transfer project,
- the goal setting for a "device system" and
- the task definitions for individual devices of the system

being derived.

For some of the devices and procedures, the following patents were created, among others:

- "Self-explanatory system analysis" US 7,698,596 and DE10351782 (Busch & Soukal, 2007, 2010),
- "System to Optimize Radiation Exposure for User and Patient" US 7,490,987 (Busch, 2009a) and
- System to calculate and communicate the "path of least resistance" through a chronic total occluded vessel DE102008031146B4 (Busch & Übler, 2012)

Fig. 3.5 An example of interdisciplinary development work, from left to right: Dr. med. Claus Christmann, Prof. Dr. Klaus Henning Busch, Dr. rer. nat. Klaus-Jürgen Kurth

3.2 Identifying and Analyzing Contradictions

In problem-solving, further development, or the development of new devices and procedures, we are often confronted with situations, especially in medical technology, where opposing desires and scientific laws or organizational conditions come into play and seemingly complicate solutions.

For instance, in imaging procedures:

- On one hand, a detailed representation of structures and processes with high resolution is desired for the best possible diagnosis and therapy, and
- On the other hand, the radiation exposure for the patient should be kept as low as possible.

For the equipment of laboratories and operating rooms:

- On one hand, the most universal hardware and software systems are desired, and
- On the other hand, the acquisition and operating costs should be kept as low as possible, and easy operability should be ensured.

Often, attempts are made to find compromises or to find an acceptable solution through optimization. Future-oriented innovation is generally only achievable by resolving the contradictions identified within the system.

We define the term "contradiction" in the context of this material as follows: A contradiction is the objective mutual relationship of two real opposites of a system or an object, which both condition each other and simultaneously exclude each other.

In the context of technical-technological development processes (innovation processes), it is crucial to identify the main contradiction, as its resolution significantly influences the solution of all subordinate contradictions (Klaus & Buhr, 1976)

The role of contradiction and its resolution already plays a role in Chinese philosophy through the concepts of Yin and Yang. Kant, Hegel, and Marx fundamentally deal with contradiction (antagonism) and its role in natural and social systems. (Klaus & Buhr, 1976)

Key Insights of the Chapter

- The diagnosis of the problem situation is the key to efficient and consistently goal-oriented problem-solving. From the recognized, but initially vaguely formulated problem situation, the diagnosis—through systematic preparation—leads to the **precise problem statement**. The **goal** of the project—i.e., the desired innovation—as well as the **available resources** and potentials, all expected **conditions**, and the desired and undesired **side effects** must be considered. **Guiding principles** support the systematic approach.

- Recognizing the contradiction underlying the problem situation reveals the mutual relationship of the internal opposites, which both condition and simultaneously exclude each other. The resolution of the internal contradiction provides the core of a patentable protection of the invention.
- For the precise elaboration of the diagnosis, it is advisable to budget one-third of the total project processing time.

References

Busch, E. (2009a). *Patent "System to optimize radiation exposure for user and patient"* (USPTO Patent 7490987). http://patft.uspto.gov/netacgi/nph-Parser?Sect1=PTO1&Sect2=HITOFF&d=PALL&p=1&u=%2Fnetahtml%2FPTO%2Fsrchnum.htm&r=1&f=G&l=50&s1=7490987.PN.&OS=PN/7490987&RS=PN/7490987.

Busch, E., & Soukal, P. (2007). *„Selbsterklärende Systemanalyse" Patent* (German Patent Office Patent DE000010351782). https://register.dpma.de/DPMAregister/pat/register?AKZ=103517820.

Busch, E., & Soukal, P. (2010). *"Medical Device for Diagnostics or Therapy" Patent (Self-Explanatory System Analysis)* (USPTO Patent 7698596). http://patft.uspto.gov/netacgi/nph-Parser?Sect1=PTO1&Sect2=HITOFF&d=PALL&p=1&u=%2Fnetahtml%2FPTO%2Fsrchnum.htm&r=1&f=G&l=50&s1=7698596.PN.&OS=PN/7698596&RS=PN/7698596.

Busch, E., & Übler, J. (2012). *"System to Calculate and Communicate the 'Path of Least Resistance' Through a Chronic Total Occluded Vessel" Patent* (German Patent Office Patent DE102008031146). https://register.dpma.de/DPMAregister/pat/register?AKZ=1020080311464.

Busch, K. H. (2003). *Innovationen erfolgreich realisieren: Erfinden lernen – lernend erfinden.* trafo.

Busch, K. H. (2009b). *Entwicklung von Geräten zum Embryotransfer bei Rindern, 64,* 442–446.

Klaus, G., & Buhr, M. (1976). *Philosophisches Wörterbuch.* Bibliographical Institute.

Koch, P. (1983). *Ausarbeiten und Präzisieren von Aufgabenstellungen, 6.*

4 Developing Solution Ideas

Abstract The number of methods and procedures for developing solution ideas is almost innumerable, and these guidelines are a fertile bunch, constantly multiplying. This chapter serves as a "compass" to practical methods of idea generation. It succeeds in breaking down the invention process into basic elements that form the building blocks of methods and procedures—similar to how elementary mathematics is based on the four basic arithmetic operations of addition, subtraction, multiplication, and division. The "basic arithmetic of invention" are analogy, variation, and combination supported by the central element, dialogue, and linked through abstraction and concretization. The analogy method, the variation method, and the combination method are described in detail and illustrated with clear examples. The deeper analysis of the methods provides the basis for their computational implementation.

4.1 Diversity of Methods

The emergence of new solutions in technology, medicine, art, politics, the military, and everyday life is often shrouded in the fog of inspiration.

However, creative work has increasingly grown out of the stage of "alchemy". Instead, experienced practitioners, scientists, and even "creativity prophets" present an almost innumerable number of methods for developing creative ideas. (Busch, 1999).

Background, Additional Information
Examples of fundamental publications are: (Busch, 1983, 1985; Busch & Busch, 2015; Busch & Krause, 1973; Fenzl, 1927; Gordon, 1961; Hansen, 1965, 1976; Hildebrand, 1969; Hill, 2018; Höhne & Koch, 1976, p. 2005; Hürlimann, 1974; Krause, 1989; Lichtenheldt, 1961; Linde, 1988; Linde & Hill, 1993; Müller, 1979; Osborn; Ostwald, 1910; Polovinkin, 1976; Werner Gruner – Life & Work, 2005).

E. Busch et al., *Methodology of Innovation*, Contributions to Management Science,
https://doi.org/10.1007/978-3-658-50010-8_4

From this multitude of methods, the following questions arise for practical work, among others:

- If mathematics, music, and some religions can manage with relatively few elements (digits, symbols, notes) and few basic rules (e.g., ten commandments, four basic arithmetic operations), can creative work—inventing—also be based on a few basic methods?
- Which idea search method is the most advantageous for a given problem?
- Is there a (universal) method suitable for all problem situations?
- Is there a system of order or a classification of methods?
- Which methods should be included in education and training?

It turns out that there is a clear contradiction between the number of mostly empirically found methods and their theoretical basis. Even a superficial review of the methods reveals that many of them bear an unmistakable similarity to each other (Busch, 1979).

This situation is extremely problematic for both the application of idea-finding methods in the innovation process and for learning oriented towards practical application.

Therefore, it is sensible and necessary,

- to provide the creative individual with a manageable number of idea-finding methods,
- that he acquires the competence to master and practically apply this manageable number of methods,
- that the acquisition of the corresponding methodological competence is taken into account in the educational concepts and curricula of vocational training and further education,
- that teachers and learning advisors have the necessary competence to convey these methods, including advice and support in the learning and work process, and
- that suitable teaching and learning materials (also using information and communication technologies) are provided.

It is necessary to break down the innovation process into elements that can be considered as basic building blocks of individual methods and thus play a similar role to molecules in chemistry.

The following will show that the basic methods of analogy and adaptation can form the basis of creative work.

These methods can be supplemented by their specific characteristics and tools, as well as by the additional operations of diagnosis, communication, and transfer (of inventions into innovations).

4.2 Identifying Analogies

4.2.1 Introductory Remarks

Identifying analogies is based on fundamental procedures of human thinking—remembering similarities and transferring them to the present situation. Analogies can be formed in various areas of technology, nature, art, or science. The formation of analogies can occur at different levels of abstraction. For example, analogies of function, structure, form, and material are possible.

The transfer of analogies from nature to technology is the special field of bionics.

The approach is based on system theory and assumes that a system has a function, a structure, and an environment. Systems thus have functional characteristics and structural characteristics. After clarifying the problem, essential functional characteristics are to be abstracted as search characteristics.

The character of analogy identification changes in the various phases of the problem-solving or innovation process. While the search for fundamental solution ideas should identify particularly distant and original analogies, closer analogies are useful for the concrete design of the solution (model experiments, similarity theory, calculation methods).

Depending on the level of abstraction and the area of analogy, either trivial or original analogies can emerge. Trivial analogies generally do not lead to inventions. The search for analogies in adjacent fields (technology, medicine, biotechnology, organization, personnel development, etc.) can be realized as an identification task at both the structure level and at least at the principle level using catalogs or databases.

4.2.2 Inspiration from Adjacent Fields

When looking for a solution to a problem, the initial questions are:

- What is already available?
- What can be adopted?

Standardized components or even ready-to-use solutions are typically “queried” from catalogs (databases) and directly adopted or adapted to the conditions of the specific problem situation through professional action.

In cases where no sufficient solution can be adopted or a completely new solution must be presented, similar solutions in adjacent (related) fields must first be identified. Such adjacent fields include, for example:

- Human medicine—Veterinary medicine
- Vehicle engines—Stationary engines

For this,

- knowledge beyond the narrow field of expertise and/or
- the use of suitable data storage

is required.

The necessary information can be obtained through.

- attending trade fairs and exhibitions,
- attending conferences and congresses,
- evaluating professional literature,
- internet research,
- patent searches, and
- discussions with colleagues from different fields of expertise.

From a patent law perspective, it should be noted that analogies should preferably be sought in distant fields. Insights from adjacent fields only lead to protectable solutions if prejudices of the professional world are overcome or if internal contradictions have to be resolved when transferring the found principle to the specific problem situation.

4.2.3 Inspiration from Nature

The search for examples from biology for product, process, and organizational innovations does not have to be left to chance. Several scientists have developed knowledge databases that support the systematic identification of solution ideas (Hans Hill, 2018; Marguerre, 1991). Pedagogically prepared material is available from Hill (Hill, 1996). Catalogs of biological structures are offered, which are ordered according to an orientation model. This orientation model is based on basic biological functions and thus facilitates the search process.

The approach to problem-solving using the analogy method is illustrated in Fig. 4.1.

4.2.4 Inspiration from Historical Sources

Fairy tales and legends are an interesting source for the development of new solutions through analogies.

Let's consider some examples.

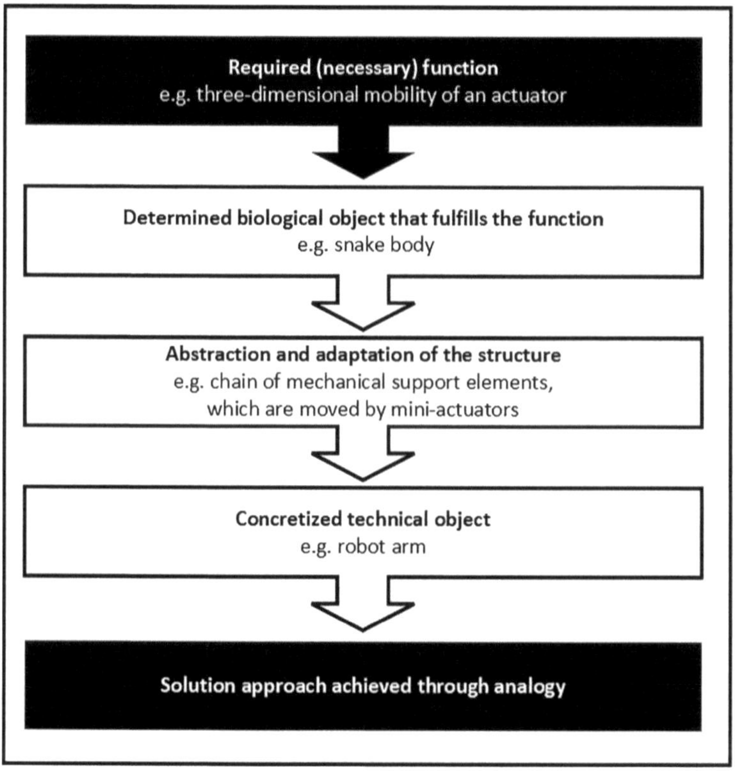

Fig. 4.1 Approach to problem-solving using the analogy method

Example

The Pied Piper of Hamelin

"In the year 1284, a strange man appeared in Hamelin. He wore a coat of many-colored, colorful cloth, which is why he was called the Pied is said to have been called, and claimed to be a rat catcher. He promised to rid the city of all mice and rats for a certain fee. The citizens agreed with him and assured him a specific wage. The rat catcher then pulled out a small pipe and blew it. Immediately, the rats and mice came running out of all the houses and gathered around him. When he thought there were none left, he went out, and the whole crowd followed him, and so he led them to the Weser. There he hitched up his clothes and stepped into the water, whereupon all the animals followed him and drowned as they plunged in." (Trommer, 1966, p. 85–86). ◀

The attraction and repulsion of rats, mice, and moles with acoustic means has been state of the art for several years and the corresponding devices can be found in many mail-order catalogs. The use of acoustic means to influence animals often appears in legends and fairy tales.

Another example is:

Example
The Little Fiddler of Wolfsbach

"Once a fiddler was going home from a church fair, where he had been playing for the people until deep into the night. The little man did not like to walk the straight path and therefore strayed so far to the side in the thick forest he had to cross that he eventually fell into a pit that the hunter had dug to catch wolves.

The shock was great enough for the fiddler when he suddenly fell from the earth down into the depths. But his horror increased even more when he landed on something alive that jumped up wildly, and when he realized it was a wolf looking at him with glowing eyes. The man had nothing but his violin in his hand. In his fear, he began to play all his little tunes in front of the open wolf's mouth, which this time did not seem funny to him at all. However, the wolf must have found the music particularly beautiful and touching; because he began to howl loudly, which probably—like our musical dogs when they hear song and sound—should be called singing.

Luckily, old Jobst, the hunter, who had heard the wolf singing from afar and only heard the fiddler playing close by, came along. He pulled the conductor out of the mouth of the hungry wolf just in time ...". (Trommer, 1966, p. 86–88).

However, the Pied Piper of Hamelin was disappointed by his clients:

"But after the citizens were freed from their plague, they regretted the promised wage, and they refused the man under various pretexts. So he left angry and bitter. On June 26, at seven o'clock in the morning on the day of John and Paul, he appeared again, now in the guise of a hunter, with a terrifying face, with a red, strange hat, and let his pipe be heard in the alleys. Immediately, this time not rats and mice, but children, boys and girls from the age of four, came running in large numbers, ... The whole swarm followed him, and he led the children into a mountain, where he disappeared with them." (Trommer, 1966, p. 86–88).

Presumably, Buntig was also the inventor of the discotheque. ◀

Even in classical antiquity, interesting suggestions for modern technical solutions can be found. Not only Daedalus and Icarus with their flight attempts play a role here.

Example

Hercules, a son of Zeus and Alcmene, had chosen the more difficult path of toil and work at the crossroads between "bliss" and "virtue". The fifth task, which was unworthy of a hero, led him to King Eurystheus.

"He was to clean the cattle yard of Augeas in a single day. Augeas was king in Elis and had large herds of cattle. His cattle were kept in a large enclosure in front of the palace, in the manner of the ancients. Three thousand cattle had been standing there for some time, and so an infinite amount of dung had accumulated over many years, which Hercules was now to remove, to his disgrace and, what seemed impossible, in a single day.

When the hero stood before King Augeas and, without mentioning anything about the order of Eurystheus, offered himself for the mentioned service, the king measured the magnificent figure in the lion's skin and could hardly suppress his laughter that such a noble warrior was lusting after such menial servitude. However, he thought to himself: self-interest has already led many a brave man astray, it may be that he wants to enrich himself at my expense. That will help him little. I can always promise him a large reward if he cleans out the entire stable for me, for he will carry out little enough in one day. Therefore, he confidently said: "Listen, stranger, if you can do this and remove all the dung for me in one day, I will give you a tenth of my entire cattle stock as a reward:"

Hercules accepted the condition, and the king thought nothing else but that he would start shoveling. But Hercules, after first taking the son of Augeas, Phyleus, as a witness to that contract, tore open the ground of the cattle yard on one side, directed the streams Alpheos and Peneos, which were not far away, through a canal, let them wash away the dung and then flow out again through another opening. Thus he carried out a disgraceful order without humbling himself to an act that would have been unworthy of an immortal." (Schwab, 1959, p. 138–139).

This made Heracles the inventor of flush away dung removal. ◀

Methodological Steps

In the context of cybernetic systems theory, all system components, including the system environment, can be the subject of analogy formation. This results in the following analogy objects:

- System
  - Structure
  - Elements
  - Relations between the elements (arrangements, couplings)

- Function
  - Transition function (input–output relation)
  - Development function
- System environment

Regarding the analogy of shape, the following characteristics can be included in the analogy formation:

- Geometry (shape)
- Material
- State (aggregate states, stress states)

Analogies can be formed at several levels of abstraction:

- Entity level
- Entity principle level
- Procedure principle level

Analogies can be found in different areas:

- Adjacent areas of the problem area
- Distant areas from the problem area
- Nature
- Art, etc.

Depending on the level of abstraction and the analogy area, either trivial or original analogies can be the result, see Fig. 4.2. This statement is in line with the eight postulates for the heuristic of analogy listed by (Busch, 1981).

Trivial analogies generally do not lead to inventions. The search for analogies in adjacent areas (of technology, medicine, biotechnology, organization, personnel

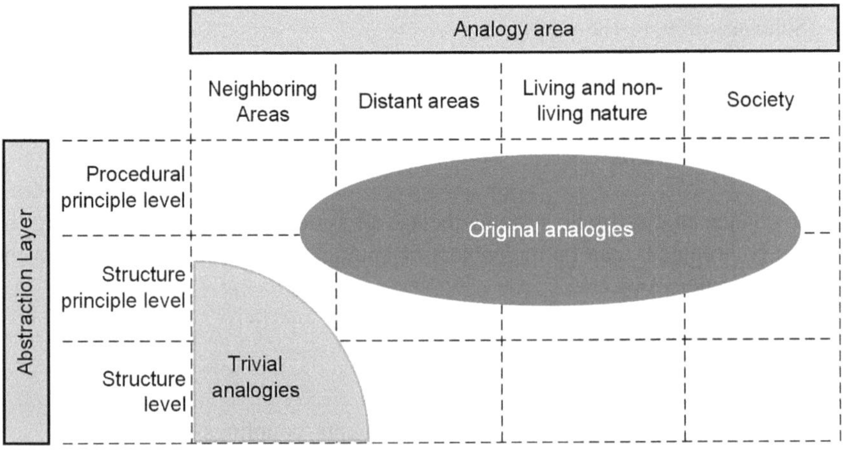

Fig. 4.2 Originality of analogies depending on the level of abstraction and the analogy area

development, etc.) can be realized as an identification task at both the structural level and at least the principle structural level using catalogs or databases.

The **general procedure** for applying the analogy method can be formulated as follows:

1. The subject of the analogy method are systems (originals) that can exist at various levels of abstraction.
2. If there is not yet a sufficient level of abstraction, it is first necessary to abstract to the characteristics essential for the problem (see Fig. 4.2). These characteristics are fixed (constant) search characteristics for the subsequent identification process (recognition of analogs). Often these are characteristics of the function. Depending on the specific problem, geometric (e.g., in product design) or material characteristics can also become search characteristics.
3. Through identification, all the systems are determined,
   - that possess the search characteristics and (in the sense of "∧")
   - that are available in the memory and (in the sense of "∧")
   - that can be captured within the available search time and (in the sense of "∧")
   - in which (upon identification by humans) a subjective identification threshold is exceeded.
4. Recognized analogical systems can either be used directly as a solution to the problem or further systematically processed.
5. The further processing of the recognized analogies into the required problem solutions can be done through the analysis of the identified systems regarding the variable features, their linkage, and their adaptation to the specific problem situation.

The **analogy method** is an approach in the problem-solving process; it is thus simultaneously a subject of learning and a working tool in the implementation of innovations.

Among other things, the following interactions arise between method application and learning process:

An effective application of the analogy method requires at least the following prerequisites:

- a thorough clarification of the problem beforehand
- a confident mastery of the methodical approach with its problem-appropriate modifications and the ability to adapt these to specific problem situations
- a broad general knowledge in scientific, technical, and artistic fields
- a pronounced observational skill
- the ability
  - to abstract and concretize,
  - to analyze and synthesize,
  - to identify (according to given search characteristics) as well as
  - to evaluate and decide (select, filter)

- knowledge about suitable knowledge repositories
- the ability to work with knowledge repositories including the potentially required media competence
- When applying the analogy method, working in groups, composed of several disciplines, can be very beneficial.

"For **learning in innovation processes**, the ability to apply the analogy method can be directly integrated into the project processing. The following approach has proven to be effective:

- Introduction to the method
- Demonstration of the methodical approach using a concrete example
- Application of the method in the concrete project processing process
- Reflection of the work and learning process
- Additional information about special cases, modifications, and meaningful adaptations
- Further learning advice

When applying the method (including the associated learning processes) in innovation processes, it can be useful to support the teacher (also in his role as supervisor and learning advisor) with external experts from the fields from which the suggestions for analogy solutions are to be obtained (accessing implicit knowledge)." (Busch, 2003b, p. 85).

Fig. 4.3 illustrates a computational implementation.

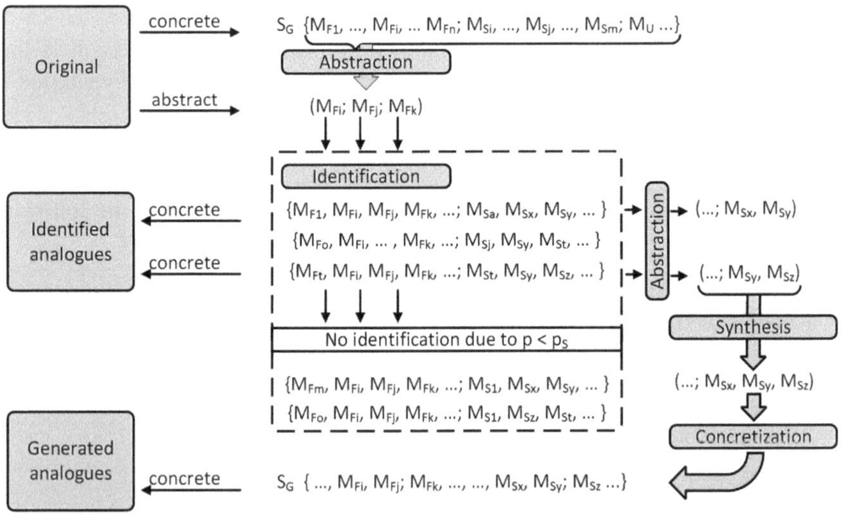

Fig. 4.3 Hypothetical schema of the analogy

Example

Example from medical technology "Minimization of X-ray dose during angiography examinations"

Short text from patent application "Visualization of catheter guidance using Augmented Reality".

The problem situation is as follows:

"Depending on the examination, guiding the catheter through the vascular system to the heart can take several minutes. During this time, X-ray radiation is used to determine the position of the catheter according to current technology." (Busch, 2008)

With the help of the doctor—as an involved partner—the following contradiction was formulated:

"X-ray radiation is harmful to the human body. Therefore, it is a fundamental concern of medical technology to reduce the applied dose while maintaining the same diagnostic and therapeutic performance." (Busch, 2008)

From this, the following task was derived:

"Find a way to visualize the position of the catheter in the vascular system with a lower amount of X-ray radiation." (Busch, 2008)

The following solution was proposed:

"The catheter is extended through a semi-transparent display that is swung over the operating field. Preoperatively generated planning and image data as well as live recorded X-ray images/series are displayed on this display. The movements of the catheter are tracked by an additional system and the position of the catheter is displayed on the display along with preoperatively generated planning and image data as well as live recorded X-ray images/series." (Busch, 2008) ◀

4.3 Adaptation of Abstract Solution Ideas

4.3.1 Introductory Remarks

The adaptation of the found suggestions to the concrete demands and conditions of the problem is achieved through:

- Variation and
- Combination.

4.3.2 Concretization through Variation

In **Variation**, improved, further developed or novel solution possibilities are derived from an existing solution through targeted, systematic changes of system properties.

Replacement	• Material exchange • Utilization of other physical, chemical, or biological effects • Application of analogical principle solutions
Addition	• Provide counterforces or pretensioning • Aggregation of elements (pencil with eraser)
Omission	• Eliminate unnecessary functions, elements, and relations • Creation of single-purpose and special devices
Disassembly	• Structuring into several subsystems (multi-stage rocket, multi-chamber tires)
Merging	• Combination of individual functions to create qualitatively new functions • Integration of functions, elements, and relations (tubular tires)
Reversing	• Swapping of stationary and moving elements

Fig. 4.4 Possibilities for qualitative modifications

Variation requires a structural analysis. All system properties can be changed, including the individual elements, their couplings and arrangements, as well as the function and environment of the system.

In addition to quantitative modifications, qualitative changes through **Replacement, Addition, Omission, Disassembling,** Merging**, and Reversal** are possible as variation operations.

Some possibilities for qualitative modifications are listed in Fig. 4.4.

"In the context of combinatorics, variation is considered a special case of combinations. From some studies on variation, it was evident that the system theory of cybernetics is an important basis for variation. Technical objects are systems. They have function and structure and are related to their environment. Systems are determined by a set of elements and a set of relations that exist between these elements. Based on previous studies by numerous authors, the following statements can be formulated about variation:

1. *The subject of variation in the context of invention methodology are ideal images of technical solutions. These technical solutions (structures or processes) are systems that are structured and can perform functions:*

$$S\left\{\vec{M}_F, \vec{M}_S\right\}$$

$\vec{M}_F$	*Set of functional features*
$\vec{M}_S$	*Set of structural features*

The structure is characterized by sets of elements $\vec{M}_E$ and relations $\vec{R}$ between these elements. Both the elements and the relations have features:

$$M_E\{M_{E1}, M_{E2}, \ldots, M_{En}\}$$

$$R\{R_1, R_2, \ldots, R_n\}$$

2. *Variation presupposes a structural analysis.*

3. *The essence of variation lies in the quantitative or qualitative change (variation operation) of characteristics M_x (objects of variation) of the elements (M_{Ei}), the relations (M_{RJ}) or the function (M_{FK}) (through memory query) as shown in* Fig. 4.5 .: *(There is a formal similarity with the Turing machine.)*
4. *Changes in characteristics usually require abstraction and concretization operations.*
5. *The application of variation operations to the objects of variation results in the variation possibilities shown in* Fig. 4.5 .

   *In Fig. 4.5 a systematization of the variation possibilities is proposed, the appropriateness of which is tested by assigning the methodological rules listed in (*Lohmann, 1960; Polovinkin, 1976*). (*Lohmann, 1960 *) provides the following measures for changing a search field, which is composed of the elements a, b, c …* (Lohmann, 1960 *, p. 1293): "We insert the elements m, s, and x at any position."*

Around 1980, the drive of artificial hearts became a current issue in medical research. The memory of the state of development at that time is characterized by the image of the American dentist who had to pull the energy and drive system for his artificial heart on a small cart.

The biological problem was technically solved at first, but the recovery of a quality of life with all the mobility desirable for a fulfilled life was not.

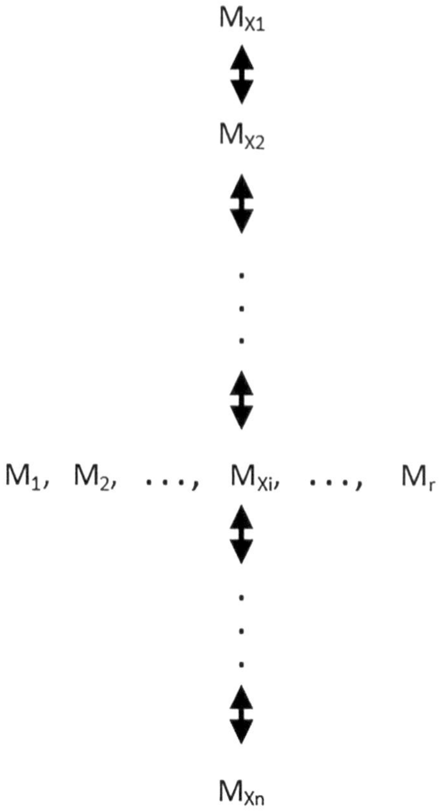

Fig. 4.5 Variation possibilities. (After K. H. Busch, 1985, p. 61)

Therefore, the task was given to medical device manufacturers to find new pumps and drive units that work energy-efficiently, are suitable for implantation, and largely avoid the mechanical destruction of blood components.

The starting point of the discussion between the physicians and device technicians were initially mechanical pump systems. The thoughts revolved around mechanical systems with electrical drive. These ideas became entrenched in the discussion, limited the search area, and formed a mental wall—a barrier.

The professional discussions were conducted in a relaxed, stimulating form, which was conducive to the development (generation) of new solution variants. Finally, the dialogue managed to jump over the limiting barrier. The idea search was extended to further areas. For the individual parts of the "artificial heart" system, more distant solution possibilities—thus new variants—were considered.

The ideas that emerged required organization. For the systematization, the system known from construction science was used, in which a device (system) is mentally broken down into its assemblies (elements) and analogical possibilities are sought for the existing assemblies or components. The functional units become variables in this methodical approach, for which variants are sought.

Using the example of the development of a device to support the blood circulation in mammals (Busch, 2003a, p. 87), the function "physiologically appropriate movement of the blood flow" was disassembled into the sub-functions.

- Energy provision
- Drive
- Pump
- Control and regulation

The sub-functions become variables for which alternative possibilities—variants—are to be found.

This resulted in the variation table shown in Fig. 4.6.

The decisive solution idea was "the body's own muscle". In multidisciplinary development work, this resulted in a patentable solution.

This approach is by no means new. As early as 1927, Fenzl presented the concept of variation using the example of press and impact tools in his book "The School of Invention". (Fenzl, 1927).

Energy	electrical	chemical	mechanical	biological
Drive	Electrical motor	Combustion engine	Muscle	
Pump	Piston pump	Gear pump	hose pump	
Control	Constant control	Dynamic regulation		

Fig. 4.6 Variations for supporting blood flow

Example

Practical example "Hazard source cable routing"

The disruptive development of Angiographic Computed Tomography (ACT) allows the creation of 3D image data directly in the angiography lab. This is advantageous for diagnosis and therapy. (Lauritsch et al., 2005).

The rapid rotation of the C-arm around the patient required for this was a new step in the treatment process. During rotation, the C-arm moves in an area under the patient table where signal cables and media lines, and in the case of general anesthesia, the respiration tube, are usually located. These cables, lines, and tubes are connections between the patient and the medical devices.

Problem situation

During the rapid rotational movement of the C-arm, these cables, lines, and tubes can be dragged along and possibly torn from the connections to the devices or from the patient. For this reason, there was a potential risk to the patient's health and the integrity of the medical devices.

This complicated the already challenging working conditions for anesthesia even further.

During the development and implementation of the ACT, the clinical environment was initially not sufficiently considered. Only through the application of the procedure in medical practice did the problem become apparent (see Fig. 4.7).

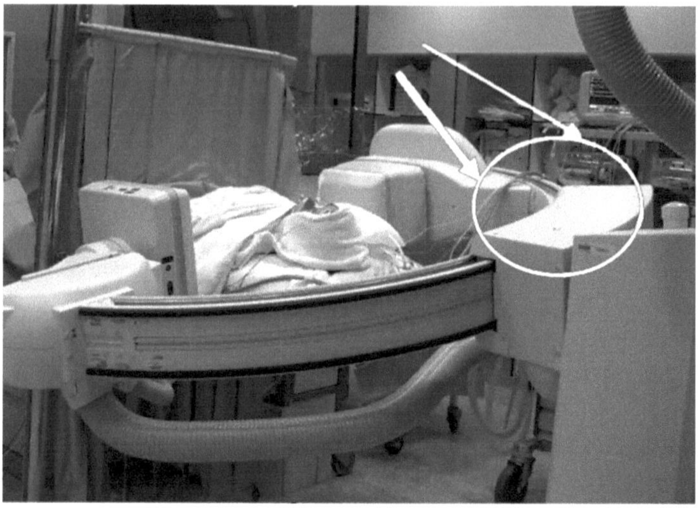

Fig. 4.7 Signal cables during rotational angiography

Impulse generator
The users formulated and transmitted the suggestions for the iterative further development.
Steps of problem-solving

- Practical solution attempts (trial and error): In a first iteration, the application specialists fixed the cables, lines, and tubes to the C-arm using bandage materials available in the lab. This solution was not satisfactory for the users.
- Order placement: Based on this feedback, the problem went through another iteration loop. After analyzing the problem, a development order was placed at the beginning. The solution to the problem, which needed to be specified, was to be carried out within the framework of a diploma thesis.
- Specification of the task: In coordination with the user, the involved colleagues defined the solution criteria, e.g., the diameter of the cables used and the required position of the cables on the angiography system.
- Disassembly: This was followed by the breakdown of the overall problem into sub-problems, e.g., positioning the cables at certain locations, minimizing the strain on the cables due to the movement of the C-arm, and ensuring quick access.
- Development of solution variants: The developers worked out different solution principles for the subtasks. The following solution methods were used: variant evaluation, variation, and dialogue method.

The **dialogue** was particularly based on brainstorming using sketches. **Analogies** were found, among other things, in the cable routing in steering columns of vehicles and in the positioning of the on-board machine gun in the propeller axis.
For the **variation** the following variation table was used (abbreviated representation in Fig. 4.8).

Variable	Variants	Assessment

Position of the cable management	• Cable routing
	  • above rotation center
	  • in rotation center
	  • floor
	  • subfloor	

Fixation of the cables	• Cable clamps • Open duct • Pipe	

Fig. 4.8 Variation table

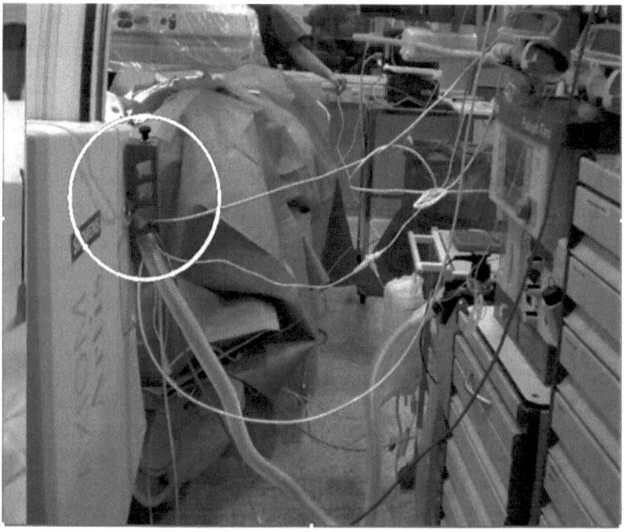

Fig. 4.9 Cable holder in the angiography lab

- Prototype construction: The functional prototype was manufactured in the prototype construction.
- Market launch: After production, the market launch followed. The preferred solution routes the cables, lines, and tubes in the isocenter of the C-arm rotation. The movement of the cables is thereby minimal.

In clinical practice, the solution depicted in Fig. 4.9 met expectations regarding patient safety and workflow for anesthesia. ◀

4.3.3 Concretization by Combining

Combining builds on variation. First, the overall function is broken down into sub-functions. Implementation variants are determined for the essential sub-functions. These variants are then to be fully or partially related to each other (combined). The combination table and the combination matrix are common forms of representation. The method of the morphological box (Zwicky, 1989) contributed to the popularization of the combination method.

The matrix representation allows the individual fields to be viewed in their context and preferred variants as well as patented or published solutions to be specially marked. This can also facilitate the development of intellectual property strategies.

From the perspective of patent law, there are restrictions that influence the protectability of the result. Variants should generally be sought in remote areas of technology or in animate or inanimate nature if a patent is sought. The combination of individual elements must lead to a surprising, unpredictable effect that realizes a technical advance. A new unified function that qualitatively exceeds the effect of the sum of the individual elements must be achieved by merging the individual functions. Aggregations do not lead to patentable solutions. The exchange of known means (screw ↔ rivet ↔ nail) does not lead to protectable solutions, as these means are considered equivalents. Patents can only be achieved if the exchange of materials or elements results in unexpected technical effects.

> "1. The subject of the combination is systems.
> 2. The system under consideration is analyzed and broken down into elements.
> 3. Relevant appearing characteristics of elements are varied. (To find new technical solutions, variants of sub-functions are primarily determined. However, all characteristics of the system and its environment can be changed qualitatively and quantitatively.) The prerequisite for the combination is that at least two characteristics are varied.
> 4. The variants are fully or partially (with restrictions) related. The preferred form of representation is the matrix (see Fig. 4.10).

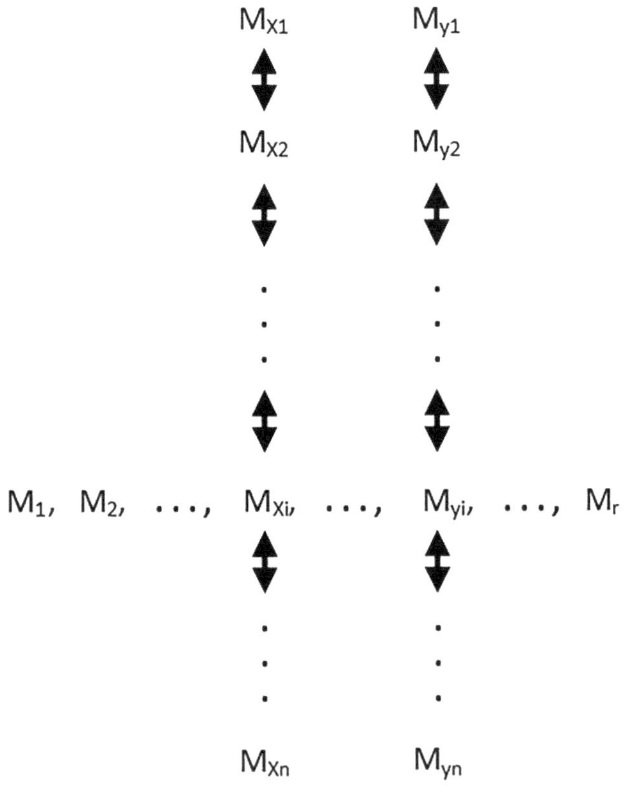

Fig. 4.10 Combination possibilities. (Busch, 1985, p. 68)

It can be seen that the set of variation operations is a subset of the combination operations." (Busch, 1985, p. 68).

Key Insights of the Chapter

- Developing ideas for solutions is based on both intuitive and systematic approaches. It turns out that from the almost overwhelming variety of known methods, procedures, rules, and recommendations, only a few **basic methods** are required for idea generation.
- The **analogy method** uses similarities to existing solutions from nature, technology, literature, and history to stimulate new ideas.
- The **variation** develops novel solution possibilities from existing solution approaches through a systematic change of system properties.
- The **combination** relates the results of the variation fully or partially to each other and preferably presents them in the form of a combination table or combination matrix.
- The identified solution ideas are to be **evaluated** with regard to the criteria identified in the diagnosis and selected for further project processing. In this project phase, in addition to economic, technical, ecological, and economic policy concerns, particular attention must be paid to intellectual property conditions (disturbing patents and utility models, opportunities for own patent applications).
- The formalization of the idea search procedures creates the basis for the idea search using **artificial intelligence** (AI).

References

Busch, B. G. (1999). *Erfolg durch neue Ideen*. Cornelsen.

Busch, E. (2008). *Patent Application "Visualisierung der Katheterführung mittels Augmented Reality"*. http://www.freepatentsonline.com/DE102006033246.html.

Busch, H. (1979). *Hierarchiches System methodologidscher Mittel In: Methodologische Probleme des technischen Schöpfertums (Russian)*.

Busch, H. (1981). *Analogie und technisches Schöpfertum*. Avots.

Busch, K. H. (1983). *Erfindungsmethodik – ein Mittel zur Effektivierung der Konstruktionsarbeit, 28th Intern. Scientific Colloquium TH Ilmenau 1983, Lecture series "Entwicklung feinmechanisch-optisch elektronischer Geräte"*.

Busch, K. H. (1985). *Methodologische Untersuchungen zum Erfindungsprozess*.

Busch, K. H. (2003a). *Innovationen erfolgreich realisieren: Erfinden lernen – lernend erfinden*. trafo.

Busch, K. H. (2003b). *Lernen in Innovationsprozessen* (Vol. 4).

Busch, K. H., & Busch, E. (2015). *Impulse der Feinwerktechnik auf den wissen-schaftlichen Gerä tebau der Agrarforschung*. TU Dresden.

Busch, K. H., & Krause, S. (1973). *Praktische Verfahren Für Die Bearbeitung Von Problemen.*, *3*, 359–371.

Fenzl, F. (1927). *Die Schule des Erfinders*. Carl Marhold Publishing House.
Gordon, W. J. J. (1961). *Synectics* . Harper.
Hans Marguerre. (1991). *Bionik – Von der Natur lernen*. Siemens Aktiengesellschaft Berlin.
Hansen, F. (1965). *Konstruktionssystematik*. Verlag Technik.
Hansen, F. (1976). *Konstruktionswissenschaft*. Verlag Technik.
Hildebrand, S. (1969). *Einführung in die feinmechanischen Konstruktionen*. Verlag Technik.
Hill, B. (1996). *Naturorientiertes Lernen*. Shaker.
Hill, B. (2018). *Bionik – Klimatisierung und Lüftung*. Knabe.
Höhne, G., & Koch, P. (1976). *Anwendung der Variationsmethode beim Konstruieren* (Vol. 25, pp. 183–186).
Hürlimann. (1974). *Probleme lösen – wie?* (Vol. 43, pp. 91–99).
Krause, W. (1989). *Grundlagen der Konstruktion—Lehrbuch für Elektroingenieure* (p. 14). VEB Verlag Technik.
Lauritsch, G., Boese, J., & Kemeth, H. (2005). Towards cardiac angiographic computed tomography. *IEEE Nuclear Science Symposium Conference Record, 2005*(4), 2350–2354. https://doi.org/10.1109/NSSMIC.2005.1596805.
Lichtenheldt, W. (1961). *Konstruktionslehre der Getriebe*. Akademieverlag GmbH.
Linde, H. (1988). *Gesetzmäßigkeiten, methodische Mittel und Strategien zur Bestimmung von Ent wicklungsaufgaben mit erfinderischer Zielstellung*.
Linde, H., & Hill, B. (1993). *Erfolgreich erfinden*. Hoppenstedt Technik Tabellen Verlag.
Lohmann, H. (1960). *Zur Theorie und Praxis der Heuristik in der Ingenieurerziehung*.
Müller, J. (1979). *Möglichkeiten und Probleme der Entwicklung der Konstruktions-wissenschaft* (Vol. 28, pp. 292–297).
Osborn, A. F. *Applied Imagination—Principles and Procedures of Creative Thinking*. Scribner.
Ostwald, W. (1910). *Die Technik des Erfindens*. Verlagsgesellschaft.
Polovinkin, A. (1976). *Methoden der Suche neuer technischer Lösungen*.
Schwab, G. (1959). *Die schönsten Sagen des klassischen Altertums*. Altberliner.
Trommer, H. (1966). *Deutsche Heimatsagen* (pp. 93–96). Der Kinderbuchverlag Berlin.
Werner Gruner – Leben & Werk. (2005). Verlag Redieck & Schade.
Zwicky, F. (1989). *Entdecken, Erfinden*. Verlag Baeschlin.

5 Communication in the Innovation Process

Abstract This chapter emphasizes that dialogue plays a central role in creative processes. The function and the problems that can arise from inadequate coordination among participants are illustrated with examples. Based on the definition of "communication", both rational and proven methods for conducting dialogue (dialogue method) as well as the development of communication in creative groups and the requirements for their leadership are described. Communication in international and globally operating multidisciplinary groups will pose new demands on their design.

5.1 The Central Role of Dialogue

In the schematic representation of operations (see Fig. 5.1) in creative processes, dialogue is not coincidentally at the center of the invention triangle. Dialogue is an indispensable element in all operations of the innovation process.

When **identifying problems**, it is not uncommon for an individual to stumble upon a deficiency that should be remedied, or a situation that could be improved. However, the impulses for solving a problem often arise from communication between several participants.

In the context of studies on the "development of biomedical devices with a large and durable base and the associated services" (Busch, 2021), it was found that both sales and customers, product management, service, and competition can act as impulse generators for new developments and further developments. The communication within the contacts of sales with the users provided more than two-thirds of the suggestions.

E. Busch et al., *Methodology of Innovation*, Contributions to Management Science,
https://doi.org/10.1007/978-3-658-50010-8_5

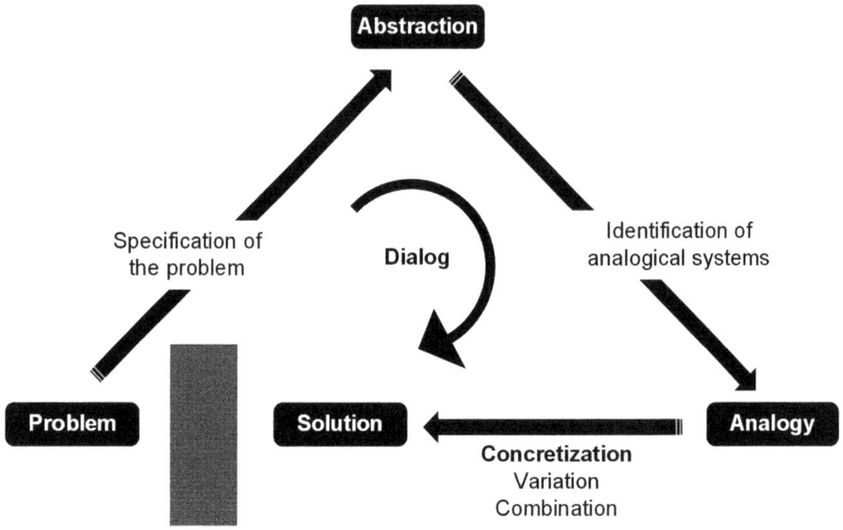

Fig. 5.1 Position of dialogue in the invention process. (Adapted from Busch et al., 2021)

5.2 The Central and Supporting Element in the Invention Process

Dialogue is also indispensable in the **clarification of problem situations**. Experience in scientific instrument construction (Busch, 2003) and in the development and further development of medical technology shows that misdevelopments often result from inadequate communication between the involved partners and thus from a deficient clarification of the problem or task.

Two simple examples should illustrate this.

Example

In the **first case**, a biologist at an institute for aquatic research submitted a sketch for a "shaking device" (Fig. 5.2) in one of the institute's workshops—with the request for prompt production.

The prompt production did not occur, as the workshop belonged to the "Scientific Equipment Construction" department and the physicists and mechanics of this department took a closer look at the order.

Over a cup of coffee (probably several), the following new—jointly developed—task was created:

To solve the research task … it is necessary for living cells to be moved in a nutrient solution to ensure favorable conditions for the ongoing life processes (especially for metabolism).

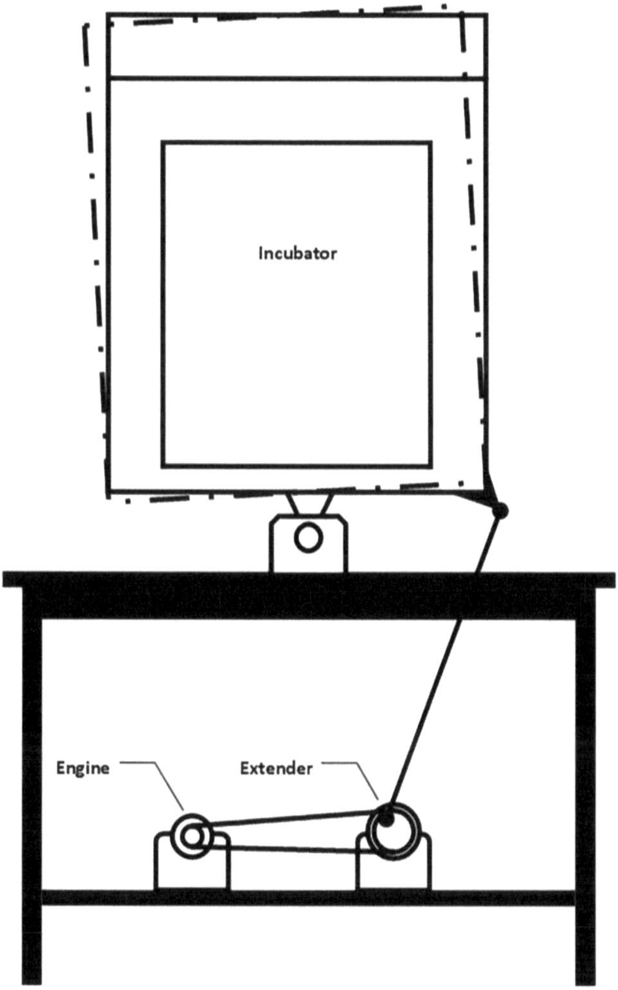

Fig. 5.2 Sketch for the desired "shaking device"

The following conditions are given:

- The cells are located with their nutrient solution in glass dishes with the following dimensions ….
- The glass dishes are positioned in an incubator with the internal dimensions …, a temperature of … + − … °C and a humidity of … %.
- The incubator has the external dimensions of … × … × … mm and a mass of … kg.

The following requirements must be met:

- Sterile conditions must be guaranteed in the incubator.
- The most favorable movement frequency is expected in the range of 1 to 10 oscillations per minute.
- The frequency must be adjustable in this range.

From the task agreed upon in collegial dialogue, the following basic principle was abstracted:

- Spherical, pressure-sensitive organic structures of … mm diameter are to be moved relative to the surrounding liquid.

Ultimately, an electromagnetically excited wobble disc was delivered and successfully used, which was introduced into the incubator. ◀

Example
In a **second example**, it is a device for testing the fitness of laboratory animals.
In joint work by biologists and mechanics, a multi-lane treadmill for working with mice (as model animals) was developed and successfully used in a research institute. The device was equipped with appropriate measurement and control technology.
During a professional conference, the interest of other research laboratories for this technology was aroused. One of these laboratories commissioned the institute workshop—as the manufacturer of the treadmill—to manufacture a device for use with model animals.
The device was manufactured and delivered ready for use.
The reaction of the employees of the receiving laboratory was sobering: "*... and how are we supposed to get our fat guinea pigs into the narrow lanes?*".
When placing the order, they simply failed to communicate sufficiently and formulate the task precisely.
A model animal is not just a model animal. ◀

In the **identification of analogical systems**, the search space is significantly expanded by the interaction of people from different disciplines and from all phases of the development and application process, thus enabling unexpected creative solution ideas.

Finally, the **concretization of the solution idea**, i.e., the adaptation of the idea to the specific area of application can only be optimally designed when a trusting dialogue is conducted between the users and the developers.

Important!
Thus, communication proves to be the central and supporting element in the entire invention process.

5.3 Basics of Communication

Under the term **communication**, we understand in this book the transmission of information between people as well as between people and computers.

The translation of the Latin word "communicare" gives the meaning "share, communicate". (We also encounter "sharing" again in social networks.)

The information can be conveyed both verbally and nonverbally.

For effective design of communication, the **communication psychology** provides important basics. (Frindte & Geschke, 2019).

Communication psychology, a subfield of psychology, is concerned with the scientific study and practical design of information exchange between individuals and within groups of people. It is therefore of interest for teaching and learning processes, training measures, and the leadership and development of organizations. Within the context of innovation processes, it forms the basis for the work of creative collectives (see section "The Special Effectiveness of Creative Groups") and international research groups.

The sender-receiver model is often used to describe the communication process (see Fig. 5.3). This model is based on a proposal by Claude E. Shannon and Warren Weaver. (Röhner & Schütz, 2015).

In the context of this book, we are interested in a particular area of communication: the **dialogue**. Dialogue generally refers to a mutually conducted conversation between two or more people.

Chains of associations are generated to initiate the linking of ideas, concepts, and other characteristics from a starting situation. The methodological elements

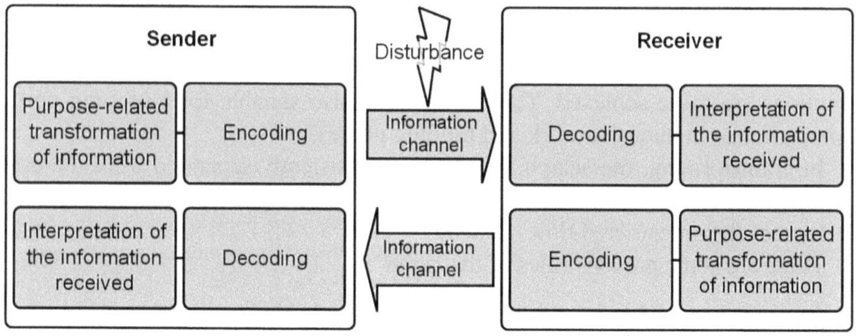

Fig. 5.3 Sender-and-Receiver Model

and other existing contents of consciousness are connected in the brain through **associations**.

For the term "associations", we use the following explanation as defined in the "Philosophical Dictionary" on pages S. 131–133:

> "**Associations** between contents of consciousness are the reflection of objectively existing relationships between things, systems, processes, etc." (Klaus & Buhr, 1976 , pp. 131–133)

The connections can be differentiated:

- by similarity,
- by contrast, and
- by spatial or temporal proximity.

Ideas can also be linked with psychological contents, such as feelings and stimulus situations.

Random associations can also be generated by computer. Computing technology offers the possibility to generate defined types of associations.

Since the chains generated by an individual increasingly move on subjectively "well-trodden paths", novel solutions are often not to be expected in the search for ideas. To prevent the narrowing of the search space, suitable methods for identifying innovative solutions can be used.

For example, if we sit in a coffee round and listen attentively, we can observe:

- One word leads to another.
- The participants go from one topic to another.

We use exactly this "digression" and "passing the ball" in the **dialogue methods** to leave well-trodden paths and overcome hurdles.

5.4 Efficient Communication Methods in the Innovation Process

A proven and frequently used method is brainstorming (the idea conference).

The use of this rational form of dialogue has proven successful in the search for solution ideas in cases where any idea is to be found—or when unconventional solutions are to be achieved. This approach is also suitable for loosening up the group climate in intensive work and training phases.

In brainstorming, the search for ideas is consistently separated from the evaluation of ideas. Special attention is paid to creating an atmosphere that positively influences the unrestricted flow of ideas.

There are some proven "rules of the game":

- For implementation, 5 to 12 "players", a "game leader" and preferably a record keeper are required.
- The duration of a brainstorming session should be 20 to 50 min.

The following procedure should be observed:

Preparation
The invitation with the announcement of the problem should be made in good time and preferably in writing. Attention should be paid to a favorable composition of the group (include experts from other areas; preferably include people of the same hierarchical level), and a suitable room (with a round table) should be selected.

Implementation
The game master initiates and announces the "rules of the game" and the problem statement.

The participants express their thoughts (No lectures! No "killer phrases"!).

The "game master" ensures compliance with the "rules of the game".

All ideas are recorded (blackboard, PC, video).

Evaluation
The ideas are reviewed and evaluated by experts. The results are communicated to the project team. The handling of copyrights must be clearly clarified before the brainstorming session.

This type of "brainstorming" can also be done in written form.

In the written variant—the **Brainwriting**—ideas are noted or sketched on prepared sheets by the participants. Of course, computing technology can also be used for this.

In a previously agreed cycle time, the results are passed on in a uniform direction to the person next to them. The noted or sketched ideas form the basis for subsequent processing analogous to brainstorming. (Busch, 2003).

5.5 The Particular Effectiveness of Creative Groups

For the effective design of creative processes, dialogue in interdisciplinary groups is of fundamental importance., cf. (Busch et al., 1985).

"Discoveries and inventions in the fields of medicine and medical technology have been predominantly developed by versatilely trained physicians over the past centuries. Their achievements often also lay in the fields of physics and technology. Some examples should prove this.

- Hermann Ludwig Ferdinand von Helmholtz (1821–1894), after studying medicine and five years of military service, worked as a professor of anatomy and physiology at the universities of Königsberg, Bonn, and Heidelberg. His achievements include the foundation of the trichromatic theory, the construction of the ophthalmoscope, and work on the theory of hearing.
- Julius Robert von Mayer (1814–1878) is particularly known for his work on the principle of energy conservation and the equivalence of work and heat.

- Ernst Alban (1791–1856) completed his medical studies in Rostock in 1814 and practiced as an ophthalmologist in Rostock from 1815. After his habilitation, he successfully worked with high-pressure steam engines. In 1829, he founded the first mechanical engineering institute in Mecklenburg and dedicated himself to the construction of agricultural equipment, shipbuilding, and the production of steam engines.
- Jean-Paul Marat (1744–1793) worked—in addition to his political engagement—as a doctor, philologist, sociologist, physicist, and publicist.
- Copernicus (1437–1543) was successful as an astronomer, mathematician, and lawyer in addition to his medical activities.
- The development of science and technology—associated with increasing specialization on the one hand and the interweaving of many disciplines on the other—created new conditions for discovery and invention in medicine and medical technology.
- As early as 1867, the collaboration of the anatomist Mayer and the engineer Culmann led to an understanding of the trajectory bone ball structure on the femoral head.
- A group of Japanese physicians and engineers provided evidence of the piezoelectric properties of bone in 1957, thus laying important foundations for further discoveries and medical technology inventions.

The modern developments in medical technology—such as artificial organs, patient monitoring systems, computed tomography, magnetic resonance imaging, or laser surgery—can only be achieved through multidisciplinary work." (Busch et al., 1985, pp. 165–168).

The state of knowledge of the natural sciences about human life processes is significantly promoted by the **multidisciplinary and interdisciplinary collaboration** between physicians and engineers. This symbiosis gives rise to new clinical-technical procedures. (Ector, 2008; Ohnesorge et al., 2002; Sferrella, 2012; Snopek, 2006).

With feedback from clinical practice, these procedures and methods are developed and refined to, for example, reduce physical and chemical side effects to a tolerable level. (Boer, 2004; Nickoloff, 2005).

Medical technology, such as angiography systems and recording systems, plays a crucial role as it is an essential tool for medical personnel in diagnostic and therapy. (Freyer, 1994).

Currently, the interfaces between disciplines have emerged as increasingly significant new research directions. Both a tendency towards deepening discipline-oriented knowledge and a clear trend towards higher complexity of research problems have become apparent. The latter requires complex solutions that can only be achieved through interdisciplinary collaboration of scientifically proven specialists oriented towards common problem and goal settings.

The differentiation of a science into disciplines, specialization, and interdisciplinarity do not mutually exclude each other, but condition each other in complex innovation projects.

In **multidisciplinary research**, partial solutions from various individual disciplines are essentially summarized or separately coordinated and condensed. Interdisciplinary research, on the other hand, achieves results that are more comprehensive, new, and unattainable with traditional disciplinary methods. This result can only be achieved through direct collaboration of various disciplines that are "networked" with each other throughout the entire problem-solving process.

Multidisciplinary work places particularly high demands on the leadership of corresponding groups and teams, as the risk of communicative misunderstandings (different content allocation of apparently same terms, different quantitative and qualitative work perceptions and methods) is large between the various disciplines and can unintentionally complicate team-building processes. Representatives of meta- and cross-sectional disciplines such as mathematicians and philosophers and experienced professionals who have successfully led international projects with representatives of various disciplines—ultimately "interdisciplinary moderators" with open ethnological-cultural attitudes and practical experiences—have advantages in leading such difficult processes.

▶ **Definition**
Innovative working groups that have reached such a level of development, we refer to—within the context of this material—as a **creative team**.

If the following question is pursued, how work groups can develop into highly efficient teams, it is assumed that not every group of people proves to be a team. In everyday life, the term "team" is often used vaguely and for any group. However, "team" characterizes a highly developed group whose members have gone through a long development process with highs and lows and continue to develop. Such a "become" team is an active group of people who have committed to common goals, work together harmoniously, and achieve outstanding performance. The members enter into close professional and social relationships with each other in order to achieve the goals binding for all with high efficiency. Successful teams also skillfully combine the special action capabilities and experiences of individual team members with a constructive team spirit. In this respect, a team is more than the sum of its members. Teamwork also stands for a "value system that promotes positive behaviors, such as listening and responding constructively to others' expressions of opinion, giving others the benefit of the doubt, supporting those who need help, recognizing the interests and achievements of others" (Katzenbach & Smith, 1998).

Team development is exciting and risky at the same time. It requires all members to be open to new ideas and to take responsibility for the development of new ideas. This is only possible through the joint struggle for progress in joint work and through the establishment of a trust basis that can also be relied on in difficult situations. An important criterion for an efficient team is finally the congruence of interests with regard to team goals and tasks and the responsible interaction of all.

Teams exist in all areas of society. The following mainly presents creative teams and their development, those who handle above-average demanding tasks in R&D and achieve creative results. And those who are supposed to implement existing creative results, i.e., bring already existing innovations into a new environment for application and possibly optimize or further develop them.

Not every group of people proves to be a creative team and thus stands out from other groups. Successful creative teams perform extraordinary achievements even under difficult conditions. The members feel responsible for the work of this highly developed group, support each other they openly discuss all the problems that stand in their way.

They skillfully combine the unique capabilities (competencies) of each member with a constructive collective spirit. Therefore, a creative team is more than the sum of its members. It is, to some extent, an emotional entity rooted in the feelings and thoughts of its members, whose well-being is particularly cared for by the members. The members form a close relationship with each other to achieve their common goals with high efficiency.

A creative team is based on a high degree of interest alignment.

The core of the team is a jointly developed value system that demands and promotes positive behaviors, especially.

- Acceptance of objections and suggestions from others, listening (as an important value) and constructive engagement with the opinions of others; critical tolerance, giving others the benefit of the doubt.
- Recognizing the interests and achievements of others and mutual support.

To reach the level of an innovative team, complex development processes are required, involving temporary confusion, disputes between group participants, many emerging questions and doubts, searching for common approaches and testing these, searching for new and creative solutions, and acceptance of these by all participants.

Fundamentally, **four phases** can be distinguished in every development of creative teams—varying in duration, intensity, and outcome:

1. Forming phase (Orientation, Formation, Getting to know each other)
   Mutual exploration, exploring different goals and expectations, uncertainties, protection needs of individual group members. Restraints, cautious and impersonal action.

2. Storming phase (Confrontation)
   Clash of different goal perceptions. Search for individual roles to assert interests. Risk of lone wolves. Conflicts between subgroups. Distance from group leader. Insistence on opinions. Open conflicts. Laborious work. Feeling of hopelessness. Beginning of the development of group norms.
3. Norming phase (Establishing consensus)
   Reduction of conflicts, new forms of interaction and behavior, feedback, confrontation on the matter. Personal involvement increases. Determination of the most important agreed goals and tasks. There is a kind of group contract (common norms). Search for identity, resistances overcome. Formation of a WE-feeling.
4. Performing phase (Cooperation)
   Stable group contract (common values), everyone is committed and identifies with the group. Creative, constructive work, flexible, open, solidary. Personal problems are resolved, roles are flexibly and functionally distributed. Free energies for task fulfillment.

Once a group has reached phase 4 and solved the tasks together and innovatively at a high level, it can take on new tasks and reorient itself, or it will be dissolved in its current form. Thus, a final phase 5 can also be spoken of:

5. Separation or Evaluation phase (Completion).
   Review of the group contract (value consensus), renegotiation or dissolution. Also possible: separation or farewell of the group.

In the context of advisory observation and evaluation of real group processes, particularly important characteristics of successful creative teams play a role, such as **goals, performance, dynamics, structure, climate, courage, and perseverance for creative problem solutions**.

Creative teams—as partly emotional beings, rooted in the feelings and thoughts of the members, can also be visually represented in their development stages. An interesting approach is to ask the group members to draw a picture of the current situation in the group at the same time, but each for themselves, in which each individual member is given a place and characterized in relation to their contribution to group development (topic for all: "How do I currently experience our group?").

From such drawings, which are evaluated and discussed with the entire group after submission, various conclusions and suggestions for the current development phase, development problems and successes can be drawn. In and through the individual drawings, more essential things are usually expressed than is possible through verbal communication alone. Below are examples of representative drawings from group members of real work groups for development phases 1 to 4 (Heyse, 1993).

They clearly convey the unity of rationality, emotionality, and the creative environment of group development. The emotional side, which is indispensable for creative processes, is often neglected in the support of group development processes, especially since many leaders are not prepared for it and prefer to keep feelings and emotions "out of the picture".

Images of the Forming Phase

The individual members are recognizable.

They are passively waiting and distant.

There are no interactions and capabilities yet.

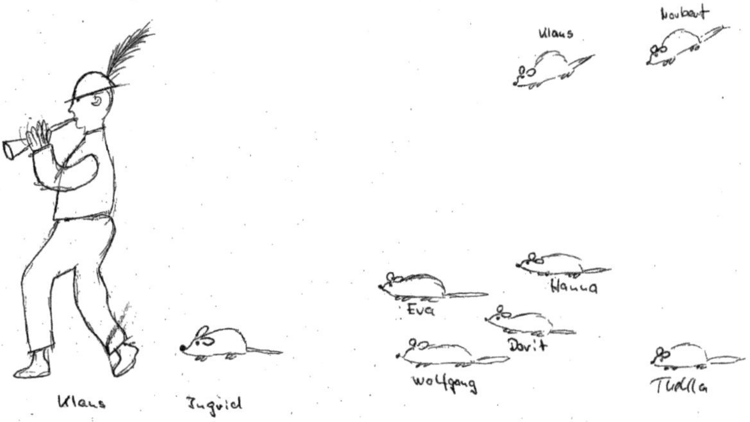

Images of the Storming Phase
Everyone is working on their own.

Here you see "Everyone is doing their own thing"—alone or in pairs. The apparent group leader remains passively above all.

Images of the Norming Phase

This includes a representation of the members in relation to the assumed “group center” (commonalities). They are viewed in a differentiated manner

a. in terms of their activity (mobile-static)
b. according to their creativity (wing sizes) and
c. according to their perceptual ability (eyes).

This is followed by a representation of the group with its presumed potential in the form of different geometric shapes and figures.

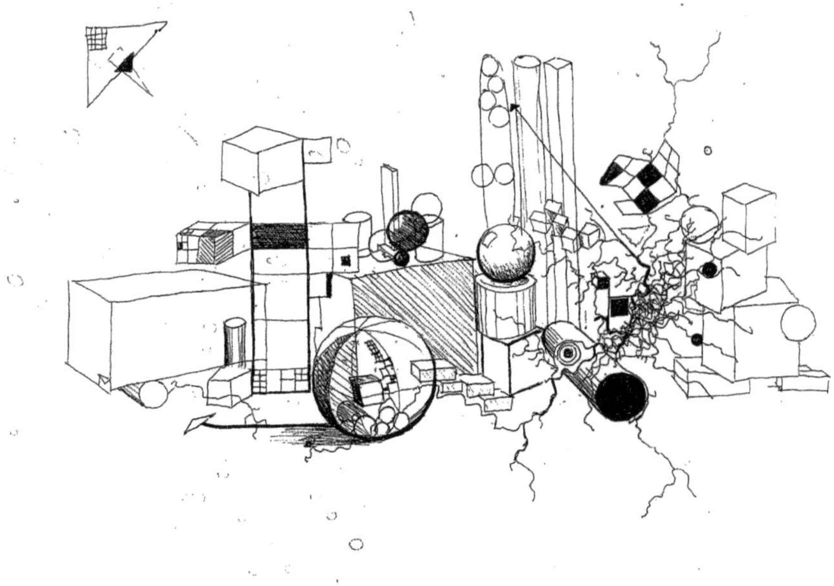

Group portrait:

Everyone is looking forward. There are no recognizable dissonances. The members are configured differently and "peaceful".

Images of the Performing Phase

The group as an orchestra with all important instruments (competencies of the participants. Some are capable of playing different instruments).

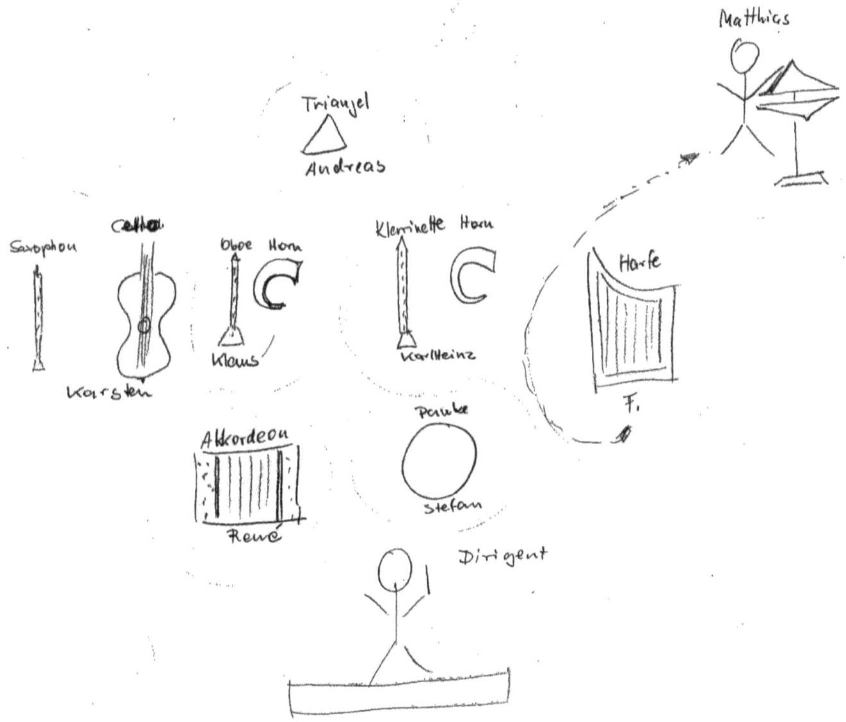

The group leaves a dark tunnel (echo of past development phases) behind.

They communicate and interact with each other.

They move forward and look ahead.

The following image shows: The team members are socially networked and show solidarity in overcoming obstacles.

The following image shows a face: productive, vibrant harmony, top team.

All members are integrated in their individuality into a common face.

and fulfill all sensory functions.

This represents the ideal state.

Important!
When re-staffing a group with the aim of creatively solving problems, for example achieving technical principle solutions or even contradiction solutions, the necessary (beyond technical) competencies and the temporary roles of potential group members should also be considered in the preparation and the personnel selection should be aligned accordingly.

In the past, roles were roughly distinguished as follows:

- Alpha role: Leader of the group
- Beta: Expert and rational supporter of the leadership
- Gamma: Led group member
- Omega: Questioner/"opponent" of the group leadership.

Today, such a classification is considered too rigid and insufficient, especially with regard to creative solutions. Instead, it is increasingly assumed that "competence clusters" are required in groups.

Definition
Competencies are understood here as self-organization dispositions of the meant as abilities to act creatively and self-organized in situations that are open to the future and problems. Such competencies are becoming increasingly important in situations that are open to problems under conditions of great political and cultural uncertainty and unpredictability, and through digitization. Disruptive upheavals require a multitude of competencies at individual, group, company, organizational, and network levels to be mastered.

In the German-speaking world, the Competency Atlas has established itself for such considerations and for concrete derivations for personnel selection, personnel development, and personnel development.

For the compilation and innovative leadership of groups and creative collectives, the following 10 competency clusters based on the Competency Atlas can provide guidance:

P: Calm Anchor, Silent Role Model

Is loyal, radiates credibility, shows personal responsibility and a clearly authentic normative-ethical attitude.

S: Team Player

Has strong communication skills, masters constructive relationship management, has strong cooperation skills and constructive adaptability.

F: Expert

Has comprehensive technical knowledge, interdisciplinary knowledge, and exhibits differentiated planning behavior.

A: Active Implementer

Radiates energy, shows initiative, is mobile and strong in execution readiness.

PA or AP: Enthusiast

Strong ability to commit, open and brave for changes, has creative abilities and is capable of self-management. Is decisive, creative, innovative, and psychophysically and socially resilient.

PF or FP: Responsible Person

Strong willingness and ability to learn, has holistic thinking ability, ability for action discipline, is reliable. Clear knowledge orientation and analytical abilities. Has strong analytical and (factual) judgment abilities. Radiates objectivity.

PS or SP

Has a sense of humor, is capable of conflict, helpful. Can integrate, is team-capable and can adapt well to cooperation partners, customers, the public.

AF or FA: Coordinator

Acts result-oriented, is goal-oriented and persistent, behaves consistently. Has conceptual strengths and organizational ability. Is diligent and characterized by a clear systematic-methodical approach.

AS or SA: Initiator

Radiates optimism, gives impulses and is quick-witted. Socially committed, strong in acquisition, experimental. Clear problem-solving and consulting skills.

FS or SF: Technical Mediator, Consultant

Ability to manage projects, awareness and responsibility for consequences, strong learning ability, external and internal technical recognition, eloquent. Communication ability, high sense of duty and conscientiousness.

Important!

Nobody is perfect. Therefore, in the context of personnel selection for new groups and a creative synergy search, discussions on the competency clusters that must be represented in the new group are essential. At the same time, it should be considered who should be encouraged or developed in certain action capabilities. The selection of the required competency clusters must of course be based on the goals and tasks of the group in its development into a creative team.

The emphasis on competency clusters as a selection and working basis for group developments becomes particularly important in internationally composed groups, in which ethnological, cultural (including educational) peculiarities should be taken into account and used. The competency view of such groups also leads to the question of how temporary or longer-term foreign group members can be sworn in to the developing value system of the group and experience and live the WE-feeling of the group and confidentiality rules personally binding. The group and the leadership of the group must also be prepared and empowered for these aspects.

In addition to the advantages and special features of creative teams listed so far, another group advantage that is far too rarely used in practice should also be pointed out: in complicated (estimation) tasks, eloquent or high-status individuals can dominate with their estimation results, even though other individuals are much closer to the true estimation results. However, if a number of individuals independently submit their quantified estimation results in writing, large individual differences can become apparent. The greater the number of independently involved individuals and statistically evaluated results, the closer the result is to the true value.

This may sound trivial, but it can provide important impulses in certain phases of problem recognition and solution—far beyond simple discussions, especially as the individual estimates can be significantly enriched by external respondents.

Background, Additional Information:

Albert T. Poffenberger (1885–1977) was an American psychologist and former president of the American Psychological Association (APA). He developed the so-called comparison figures with different surface areas (Hofstätter, 1973).

Perception psychological studies according to Poffenberger started with ten comparison figures with different surface areas, some of which had barely perceptible differences to the naked eye and without measurements. The test subjects were to

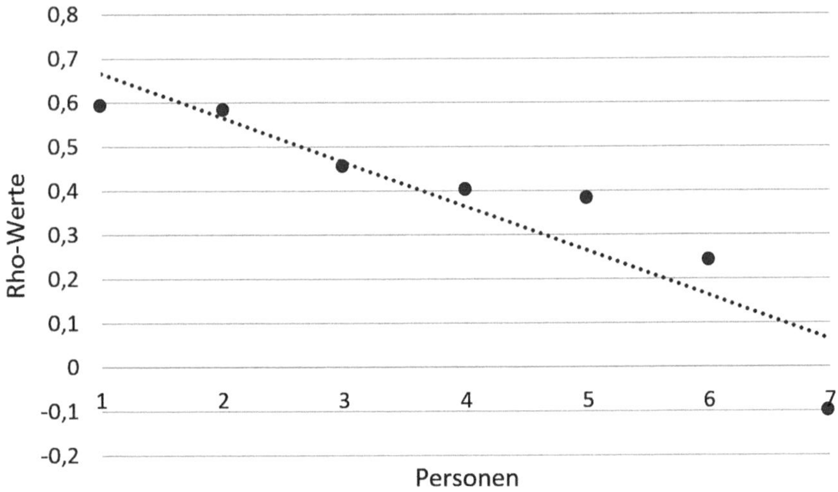

Fig. 5.4 Correlation between the rankings of the test subjects and the actual surface area. Number of deviations from the real values approaching zero

individually—separate from the other participants—develop a ranking from the figure with the largest surface area to the one with the smallest. He then correlated the rankings of the test subjects with the actual surface area.

In the Fig. 5.4 the synthetic values are illustrated using the example of 7 test subjects. Similar trends were repeated in numerous studies. The number of people with the "best estimates" is certainly of interest to the group, but more so the increase in estimation accuracy with the increase in test subjects. However, the increase in estimation accuracy with a number of more than 10 individual estimates is only marginally noteworthy. The results of these studies are representative of a wide variety of estimates and have almost universal applicability.

Now the question arises as to the characteristics of an exemplary successful ("ideal") group development at the level of a creative team.

Characteristics in detail at the end of development phase 4:

Tasks and Goals

They are clear to all members and are agreed upon. Controversial points are discussed openly and with the involvement of all members, and solutions are sought together. These are also jointly represented to external third parties.

Task Processing

The processing begins with clear requirements and acceptance by all members. Responsibilities are taken seriously, and there is feedback within the group on the nature and result of their perception.

Communication
Communication is clear and open, spontaneous and accessible to all members. Through unbiased listening among members, important ideas are heard by all. Anything that benefits the group can be communicated. Information is given even without being asked. There are no individual fearful communication blockages and restraints.

Group Self-Reflection
The group is constructively critical of itself. It monitors its work, functionality, and interaction, discusses difficulties openly, and seeks solutions together.
Criticism is constructively, openly, and fearlessly represented, and it is not perceived by the other group members as a personal attack or personal evaluation of the person. Constructive (!) criticism also brings the views of the speaker to better solutions for discussion. It is intended to illuminate and help overcome existing obstacles.

Group Climate
It is largely relaxed and optimistic. Mutual respect and spontaneous, result-oriented, unbureaucratic interaction with each other contribute to the well-being in the group. The group identifies with the tasks and also with the possibilities of exchanging experiences among each other and with the expansion of their own competencies.

Feelings
Feelings are shown as far as they concern the group goals and contribute to problem solving. Everyone should know what the other group members think and how they think about each other. Feedback on the matter and on personal contributions is given spontaneously and constructively and is also demanded.

Disagreements
Different individual opinions are accepted and heard by the group. Dissonances and conflicts are not perceived as disturbing from the outset, but as challenges for further discussion and consultation. One of the basic principles is: conflicts help the group progress and must be constructively resolved away from personal rivalries and individual interests at the expense of the group.

Decisions
The group examines the consequences of potential decisions (factual, social) and prepares decisions in the spirit of consensus in the group. Everyone must agree to the targeted solutions and the ways to achieve them. Concerns are presented openly and precisely, discussed, and largely taken into account in the decision.

Group Leadership
The individual goals and interests of group members are merged with the team's objectives. The members essentially embody a form of entrepreneurship.

Leadership is viewed and perceived as a collective responsibility. There is a fundamental understanding among all members to take on responsibilities independently and to assume other responsibilities and duties as required.

If the collective action is aimed at addressing societal core issues that are to be solved more quickly and effectively than by other groups—nationally and internationally—a common language among the various specialists develops rapidly.

This common language is further shaped by a jointly created multidisciplinary **minimum concept network** and by the jointly applied methods (structural scientific, special investigative, and problem-solving methods). The terms born and formulated with a "common language" (at a higher level of abstraction) lead to a significantly expanded research field.

Creative Teams—Where is the Future of Work Heading?

When seriously considering the requirements for future creative leadership and competence development in the context of digital transformation, many questions arise, the answers to which directly and indirectly have a significant influence on the development and deployment of creative teams, for example:

- Does the company's management see it as a core task of the executives to convey the purpose and company goals in an understandable and action-oriented manner and to form temporarily limited high-performance teams from a variety of specialists? Or do such notions and " SALUTation " still prevail as "SUPERvisor" or "CO-worker"?
- Are flat hierarchies prevalent in the company, or do innovative proposals get lost in a "chain of command"?
- Are radical ideas allowed to truly be creative and innovative as a company?
- How is the ability to create values and meaning in the company developed at the group and team levels? What about creativity and innovation? How far is the ability developed (and desired) to generate new knowledge and problem solutions from existing ones?
- To what extent is there experience in developing intercultural competence—and how is this lived and generalized in the company? (Heyse, 2018)

Executives increasingly take on roles as digitalization managers and identity enhancers. In creative TOP teams, different members take on leadership roles depending on the requirements and must be prepared accordingly.

The team members, as highly qualified specialists from different disciplines, can belong to several temporary teams in their own company as well as in other companies—nationally and internationally—and face a multitude of new or expanded requirements:

- International communication and work experience/mastery of foreign languages (English, French, Spanish, Russian…).
- High identification with the companies and absolute confidentiality towards third parties.

- Peer-to-peer work methods, experience exchange "one for many"—nationally and internationally. Complex division of labor, regional experts, and consultants.
- To strengthen the team: Commissioning instead of hiring: Purpose- and time-related expert support internally/externally.
- Machines as "colleagues", cooperation partners, controllers.
- Non-linear thinking as a human domain: Digital manager, experimenter, and innovator.
- Self-management as a core qualification and key competence.

For the conscious promotion of independence, self-responsibility of members of creative teams, it is fundamental that also the team-external executives.

- behave decently, inspire trust, accept employees, and do not "lead by humiliation" and degradation—and instead distance themselves from the still prevalent culture of mistrust with fear hierarchies;
- force themselves to communicate more about upcoming problems and possible solutions in the work process and, on the other hand, become more understandable in oral and written communication and convey the most important messages quickly, unencrypted, understandable, and motivating to all employees.

Teams Must Be Consciously Supported in Thinking Less About Simple Improvements and More About Questioning the Status Quo.

> "We are on the path to a world where incredible complexity is hidden behind a surprisingly simple facade." (Sumang Liu)

The effect of collaboration in groups—even in special situations—plays a particularly important role in expeditions, disasters, and space travel.

The following examples aim to illustrate communication and collective action in social structures and creative teams.

Example

First Example: The Hanseatic League.

From the middle of the twelfth to the middle of the sixteenth century, the Hanseatic League became the carrier of innovation transfer in an economic area that extended from Russia and Northern Europe to Italy. (von Schlötzer, 1851).

Successful economic cooperation across multiple cultural and linguistic areas and different forms of government required from the actors.

- proficiency in multiple languages,
- knowledge and respect for different cultures and legal systems,
- the ability to successfully conduct negotiations and sales talks,
- and the ability to safely transport goods along trade routes.

In addition to the transfer of goods, there was an exchange of knowledge about the partner regions, the adoption of technical solutions and craft procedures, the adoption of legal regulations (including Lübeck law), and suggestions for the design of regional education systems. The language development in the Baltic Sea region was particularly influenced by international cooperation. Low German was not only spoken in the German communities in many cities, but also had a significant influence on the respective national languages. It is estimated that about a third of Swedish words are of Hanseatic origin. This particularly affects crafts, mining, and trade. (Dollinger, 2012).

The economic and cultural conditions of international activities also had to be adapted to the learning culture in the Hanseatic cities. In addition to thorough training in German and arithmetic, it was necessary to acquire knowledge in the Nordic languages as well as in English, French, and even Italian. The school system had to adapt to these requirements.

Contacts with merchants from partner cities already prepared children and young people for their later tasks. Activities in the Hanseatic League's foreign offices were particularly formative for professional development.

The requirements for international cooperation competence at that time are still quite relevant today:

- "common values and norms, but at least the acceptance of the value and norm systems of the partners,
- knowing and accepting the culture of the partner regions while preserving one's own culture,
- knowing and observing the legal systems of the partner regions,
- the confident mastery of a common language and
- mastering at least basic knowledge in the languages of all partner regions,
- the ability to conduct communications in a targeted and effective manner,
- the ability to manage conflict situations and transform them into a cooperation-friendly climate for the future,
- the intention to shape cooperation for mutual benefit ("A very good deal is a bad deal."),
- the endeavor to stabilize cooperation through joint projects and develop common strategies,
- the orientation towards sustainable—stable over a longer period—cooperation and
- the sensible use of one's own resources and the resources of the partner regions (avoiding "overexploitation")." (Busch, 2005)

The Thirty Years' War devastated the Hanseatic trade area. An orderly flow of goods was no longer possible or was greatly hindered. In 1669, the last Hanseatic Day of the historical Hanseatic League took place in Lübeck. ◀

Example

Second example: The development of accessory rails for an angiography system.

The problem situation is as follows:

> "The professor and his student stood side by side at the patient table during the procedure. This is common in training situations.
> The control modules of the angiography system had been positioned very far towards the head using the movable accessory rails. As a result, both did not have enough space to stand comfortably side by side." (Busch, 2008)

The doctor—as an involved partner—formulated the following problem note:

> "When we (professor, student) stand together at the patient table , we can't get close enough to the patient. We need a longer accessory rail." (Busch, 2008)

The following cause was identified in the dialogue:

> "The example given illustrates the clinical requirement for a solution to secure the patient's arms during the examination. The user's approach was pragmatic, but as he expressed, it leads to new problems. Upon closer examination and analysis of the user requirement, a different solution approach emerged.
> The patient's arms were tied to the movable accessory rail because the supplied armrests were inadequate. However, the arms had to be secured during the long examinations (up to 6 hours)." (Busch, 2008)

The following task could be derived from this:

> "Find a solution to comfortably secure the patient's arms even during longer examinations.
> It must be easy and quick to use and not cost the user more than 500 US dollars." (Busch, 2008)

The following solution was proposed:

> "The armrest is used for lateral positioning of the arms and is slid under the patient." (Busch, 2008) ◀

Example

Third example for product definition: Collision protection for angiography systems from medical technology.

The problem situation is as follows:

> "Angiography systems are equipped with safety devices that protect the patient and the user. This includes the collision protection, which slows down the device movements when approaching the area where the patient lies." (Busch, 2009)

The doctor—as an involved partner—formulated the following problem note:

> "The collision protection is too sensitive. Turn it off" (Busch, 2009)

The following cause was identified by the developer:

> "The collision protection was not correctly calibrated." (Busch, 2009)

The following task could be derived from this:

> "Find a solution that allows easy calibration of the collision protection by the service." (Busch, 2009)

The following solution was implemented:

> "Adjustment of the installation instructions" (Busch, 2009)

The example given illustrates the clinical requirement for functionality. However, the actual problem did not originate in the development of the collision protection, but in the design of its configuration, as the calibration by the service technician was incorrectly performed. ◀

Example

Fourth example: The work of the Creativity Training Center (ctc).

Innovative activities for the development of innovation capability took place between 1986 and 1990 at the Bauhaus Dessau with its rich tradition.

After approximately fifty years of use as a vocational school, the Bauhaus in Dessau was thoroughly reconstructed and returned to the care and preservation of the Bauhaus tradition and further education. In this context, educational measures were also carried out—as a joint project of the Buidling Academy and the Carl-Zeiss-Jena combine to promote talented specialists from both institutions and later various other national companies. The commitment of *HEYSE*, who founded the "Creativity Training Center" in 1982, played a crucial role. In the following years, these training courses were continued as international courses at the Bauhaus Dessau, in which specialists from Romania, Yugoslavia, Hungary, Poland, Bulgaria, Czechoslovakia, and Latvia, as well as engineers from Austria and the Federal Republic of Germany, participated from 1988 onwards.

Learning and working were carried out on real research projects.

Among the jointly tackled projects were, among others.

- window design for high-speed trains under extreme climatic conditions,
- processes in the glass industry,
- exhaust gas purification in coal-fired power plants, and
- high-resolution digitization.

Colleagues in Riga, Moscow, and Kiev were interested in collaborating with German partners. They had extensive experience in creativity techniques, including their computer-aided development and technical application. From 1977 to 1989, for example, several joint scientific articles with Heinrich Busch were published in Latvian, Russian, and German, and further work results were mutually used. (Busch, 1979, 1981; Busch & Busch, 1980, 1983; Kurth et al., 1981).

The multidisciplinary work in the training groups tied in with Bauhaus traditions. The courses were based on the integration of creativity psychology, creativity methodology, medicine, patent law, and innovation methodology (Heyse, 1984) and realized the following principles:

- The unity of scientific-technical and social creativity was realized.
- To successfully initiate and realize innovations, the ability to recognize problems in time and the will to solve them were developed.
- Participants were provided with a methodological toolkit and social creativity to realize the ideas.
- The training was carried out on real research and development topics.
- The courses were organized in the unity of lectures and independent exercises.
- The unity of group work and individual problem-solving was ensured.
- Intuitive and systematic approaches were intertwined in the processing strategies.
- The respective processing strategy is based on a few basic methods (module system).
- The unity of real problem-solving and the development of group dynamics was consciously controlled and analyzed.
- Health promotion and leisure activities were integrated into the training program.

The unity of methodology and psychology was ensured in each training group (see Fig. 5.5) through the direct collaboration of two trainers, a methodologist, and a psychologist. Project-integrated learning practices were used, which are closely related to situated and constructivist learning.

The problem-solving process is inseparable from learning processes.

Both formal learning in courses and seminars and informal and implicit learning are found as forms of learning in innovation processes.

Informal learning plays a special role in innovation processes. It is not pure experiential learning. Theoretical foundations from both personal memory and external information are incorporated.

Our own research results suggest that the Formal learning in courses (and at conferences) only accounts for about 5% of learning in innovation processes. The remaining 95% is roughly evenly divided between informal and implicit learning. However, the proportions in funding policy and traditional

Fig. 5.5 The ctc faculty in front of the Bauhaus in Dessau

continuing education research show a reverse relationship; resources and potentials are almost exclusively focused on formal learning.
By merging project work and learning, as well as work and learning organization, favorable conditions are created for continuous current motivation within the framework of insightful learning.
Studies on learning in innovation processes clearly show that task-oriented and workplace-related learning are evolving into project-integrated learning. The acquisition of skills is integrated into the specific innovation process.
Project-integrated learning is the acquisition of professional competencies (as individual memory possessions) within the framework of specific innovation projects, which cause a behavioral change in the learners. (Busch et al., 1985).
The course included a comprehensive prevention program under constant medical supervision to manage physical and mental stress (Concentrated relaxation methods).
The courses within the framework of the ctc (see Fig. 5.6) were characterized by work in multidisciplinary creative groups. Interdisciplinary research and design can achieve such results that are more comprehensive, new, and unattainable with traditional discipline-oriented methods for each individual discipline. (Busch et al., 1985). ◀

Fig. 5.6 Seminar in a ctc course

Key Insights of the Chapter

- Communication creates the prerequisite for the competencies of several people to be bundled in the innovation process. This provides more knowledge, experience, and skills than the sum of the competencies of the individuals, as the **process-integrated dialogue** creates a **group effect** that constantly triggers new impulses for the association chains in idea finding. The dialogue already ensures a more complex approach and a higher level of certainty in defining the objectives for the innovation project.
- In addition to spontaneous dialogue, rational methods—such as **brainstorming**—are available for intensive phases of group discussion.
- The intensity and effectiveness of communication in the project group is determined by its size, personnel composition and the state of **group development**. To reach the development stage of **innovative groups**, complex development processes are required, involving disputes between group members, searching for common approaches as well as searching for new and creative solutions and acceptance of these by all participants.
- The current and further expected development towards **international multidisciplinary groups** in research and in product and process development increasingly places high leadership demands on innovation management. In this context, the importance of **communication psychology** is increasing.

References

Boer, A. (2004). *Radiation Safety during Interventional Procedures*. Optima Grafische Communicatie.

Busch, E. (2008). *Guest lecture "Signal- und Bildgebung im interventionellen Herzkatheterla bor" Lecture Summer Semester TU Dresden, IBMT.*

Busch, E. (2009). *Guest lecture "Signal- und Bildgebung im interventionellen Herzkatheterla bor"* . Summer Semester TU Dresden, IBMT, Dresden.

Busch, E. (2021). *Dissertation "Optimierung des Innovations- und Entwicklungsprozesses von bio medizintechnischen Geräten"* .

Busch, E., Bulitta, C., Nobach, K., & Strobel, N. (2021). Innovation & Entwicklung im globalen Wettbewerb. *MED engineering, 4* , 56–58. https://med-eng.de/2021/10/28/innovation/.

Busch, H. (1979). *Hierarchiches System methodologidscher Mittel In: Methodologische Probleme des technischen Schöpfertums (Russian).*

Busch, H. (1981). *Analogie und technisches Schöpfertum.* Avots.

Busch, K. H. (2003). *Innovationen erfolgreich realisieren: Erfinden lernen—lernend erfinden.* trafo.

Busch, K. H. (2005). *Internationale Kooperationskompetenz., 16*, 27–28.

Busch, K. H., & Busch, H. (1980). *Ideensuchverfahren im technischen Entwicklungsprozess.*

Busch, K. H., & Busch, H. (1983). *Systeme methodologischer Mittel der technischen Heuristik Riga (Russian)* . Snanie.

Busch, K. H., Christmann, C., & Heyse, V. (1985). *Problemlösen in interdisziplinären Kollektiven. 6*, 165–165 ff.

Dollinger, P. (2012). *Die Hanse*. Alfred Kröner.

Ector, J. (2008). *New Three-Dimensional Fluoroscopic Imaging Applications to Support Radiofrequency Catheter Ablation of Atrial Arrhythmias* [K.U.Leuven]. https://limo.libis.be/primo-explore/fulldisplay?docid=LIRIAS1669896&context=L&vid=Lirias&search_scope=Lirias&tab=default_tab&lang=en_US&fromSitemap=1.

Freyer, R. (1994). *Lehrmaterial zur Vorlesung Biomedizinische Technik.* TU Dresden.

Frindte, W., & Geschke, D. (2019). *Kommunikationspsychologie*. Beltz.

Heyse, V. (1984). *Grundlagen des wissenschaftlich-technischen Schöpfertums in Forschungs- und Entwicklungsprozessen* (Multilingual ctc-Documents), Berlin and Jena.

Heyse, V. (1993). *Berater-Toolbox „Teamentwicklung, Gruppendynamik" (DIC-Trainings- Unter lagen).*

Heyse, V. (2018). Kompetenzentwicklung 4.0 als Voraussetzung einer erfolgreichen Umsetzung von Digitalisierungsstrategien im Mittelstand 4.0. In J. Erpenbeck, S. Ortmann, & S. Coester (Eds.), *SMEs 4.0—Eine digitale Herausforderung. Führung und Kompetenzentwicklung im Spannungsfeld des digitalen Wandels.* Waxmann., Münster.

Hofstätter, P. (1973). *Sozialpsychologie*. Walter De Gruyter.

Katzenbach, J. R., & Smith, D. (1998). *Teams. Der Schlüssel zur Hochleistungsorganisation.*

Klaus, G., & Buhr, M. (1976). *Philosophisches Wörterbuch.* Bibliographisches Institut.

Kurth, J., Busch, K. H., & Busch, H. (1981). *Rechnergestützte Prinziperarbeitung in der Gerätekonstruktion* (Vol. 11, p. 492).

Nickoloff, E. (2005). *Radiology Review—Radiologic Physics* . Elesvier Saunders.

Ohnesorge, B., Becker, C., Flohr, T., & Reiser, M. (2002). Multi-slice CT in cardiac imaging. *Springer*. https://doi.org/10.1007/978-3-540-49546-8.

Röhner, J., & Schütz, A. (2015). *Psychologie der Kommunikation*. Springer.

von Schlötzer, K. (1851). *Die Hansa und der Deutsche Ritterorden in den Ostseeländern / Verfall und Untergang der Hansa und des Deutschen Ordes in den Ostseeländern.* BMA-Verlag Wiesbaden.

Sferrella, S. (2012, December 28). *Equipment service: Total cost of ownership* . Technology Management. https://www.radiologybusiness.com/topics/technology-management/equipment-service-total-cost-ownership.

Snopek, A. (2006). *Fundamentals of special radiographic procedures*. Saunders Elsevier.

6 From Invention to Innovation

Abstract An invention has achieved a significant result. This achievement—as significant as it may be—is initially just the starting permission for another challenging hurdle race, which should ideally end with a successful introduction to the market. To support and encourage this new challenge, we will present ten rules of innovation in this chapter. A necessary prerequisite for achieving an innovation is professional project management, coupled with an effective management control system. However, it should first be estimated what chances of success the innovation could have on the market and which strategy for its realization is sensible and promising. A market growth-market share matrix can serve as a decision-making tool. This matrix can simultaneously serve as a basis for developing an intellectual property protection strategy. The work of protecting rights is significantly facilitated if an appropriate infrastructure is available, in which both patent engineers and patent attorneys are involved. In many cases, it is advisable to first test the mode of operation of the proposed innovation with a sample or functional model. This allows important conclusions to be drawn for the continuation of this project, and misdevelopments can be more easily excluded in advance. A particular hurdle on the way to market introduction is the approval of the products. This applies to both the clinical approval of medical devices and the general CE marking. The preparation for the approvals is not a one-time action, but extends through all phases of product development. The most important criterion for whether an idea becomes an innovation is decided when moving from the manufacturer to the user. The decision is made in the step from manufacturer to user. The necessary implementation and distribution include both marketing and sales, as well as service. Accompanying all steps from recognizing a problem to introducing a product to the market, is the acquisition of the necessary innovation competence among all involved actors. Lifelong learning and project-integrated competence acquisition play an important role in this. Learning, in turn, requires the availability of suitable teaching and learning materials as well as the creation of conditions conducive to learning. In this chapter, practical experiences from the authors' long-standing research and design work are conveyed.

E. Busch et al., *Methodology of Innovation*, Contributions to Management Science,
https://doi.org/10.1007/978-3-658-50010-8_6

6.1 Goal Orientation and Will to Succeed

Finding an idea for an improvement, for an original product, or for a new procedure can evoke joyful emotions or even pride in one's own achievement. However, with the idea, only half the journey is completed, sometimes the journey ends at this point and the creative thought is "put on ice".

Important!
An invention only becomes an innovation when the idea has been successfully implemented in practice and has established itself in the market.
See Sect. 1.4.

One of the most famous personalities who were able to successfully build and consistently use the bridge between invention and innovation was Thomas Alva Edison. His life, his working methods, and his successes are detailed in volume 4 of the "Propyläen Technikgeschichte" (König, 1997).

His results include over 2000 inventions, of which over 1000 were protected in the USA and over 1200 internationally.

Far more significant is the transformation of inventions into marketable products (Conrad, 1980).

Particularly well-known are the perfection of the light bulb, the phonograph, the establishment of electricity works, and the entire system of electricity distribution. Edison was thus one of the most important innovation managers who thought in entire systems, had an eye on international markets, organized intensive marketing, and implemented ideas that were "left lying" by other inventors.

It is of little benefit to discuss where and by whom significant ideas were first developed, which were only later realized worldwide (and also economically effective) by Edison.

Tip
For our economic and societal development in Europe we should—in addition to venerating our poets and thinkers—also highlight and promote the "doers"!

Based on international experiences, the creativity rules proposed in Chap. 1 can be supplemented by the following innovation rules.

Definition

First Innovation Rule
Evaluate your ideas in terms of their feasibility and their **technical-economic and societal impact** comprehensively and critically!

Also use the **technology impact assessment** and the classification of the idea into higher-level systems.

Second Innovation Rule
Trust in your idea and your decision about the feasibility of your idea and develop a strong will to implement them!

Third Innovation Rule
Don't be discouraged by initial stumbling blocks!

Every failure provides you with important experiences and opens up new opportunities.

Fourth Innovation Rule
Use the **trustful collaboration** with people from other disciplines and with legal protection experts!

Keep in mind the inseparable connection between technology and economy!

Fifth Innovation Rule
From the outset, consider the **international market** and the possibilities of an **international cooperation**!

Consider the dynamics of political, economic, and environmental developments!

Sixth Innovation Rule
Create a suitable infrastructure and integrate yourself into regional, national, and international networks! If necessary, build your own networks!

Seventh Innovation Rule
Organize the **marketing** continuously from the beginning and for all work steps using all (modern) possibilities!

Involve representatives of the press selectively and purposefully in a trustworthy manner (and with respect to necessary confidentiality and patent law) in the developments.

Eighth Innovation Rule
Note that many steps in the innovation process may require new competencies from the participants.

Ensure a forward-looking **competence development and personnel development** for this! Also consider cooperation with relevant educational institutions.

Ninth Innovation Rule
Remember that every innovation (especially basic innovations) can trigger a chain of **subsequent innovations** and continuous improvements.

Use your knowledge advantage to anticipate solutions in the overall system and secure your **rights to it**.

Tenth Innovation Rule
Appreciate the achievements of all participants and the ideas and experiences of those who have made preliminary contributions! Your own merits are not overshadowed by this, but are recognized in full.

A key success factor for the realization of innovations is an integrated management control system, which is presented in the following section.

6.2 Management Control of Innovation Activities

New competitors, complex environmental conditions, and increasingly individual customer wishes challenge companies to turn innovative ideas quickly, cost-effectively, and reliably into **customer-oriented products or services**. In addition, companies must continuously look for innovative solutions to **optimize resources** and **improve business processes**.

Important!
This requires professional **innovation and project management**, which ensures both a strategically sensible selection of innovation projects and successful project execution (Fischer et al., 2015).

After analyzing the innovation potentials, companies must first identify the fields that can contribute most to increasing competitiveness and generating new competitive advantages. On these fields, **projects must be initiated, planned, and efficiently executed** promptly.

Important!
In this context, the **management control of innovation activities** as a separate area of innovation management plays an essential and overarching role (Horváth et al., 2020).

The following will therefore examine **how management control** of innovation activities **should be designed** to support the implementation of creative ideas into products or services, business processes and resources as effectively and efficiently as possible. The following questions will be answered in detail:

Overview
- What goals and tasks are pursued with management control of innovation activities?
- At what levels should management control of innovation activities be applied?
- How can innovation be managed holistically at the company and portfolio level?
- What tools can be used for management control of individual innovation projects?

6.2.1 *Objectives and Tasks of Innovation Management Control*

Management control of innovation activities deals with the **cross-functional control** of all innovation activities within a company. The tasks of innovation management control therefor go far beyond pure performance measurement in the R&D sector. The control activities primarily serve to support innovation-related management decisions and ensure transparent communication of information in the innovation process.

Definition

The control logic for innovation processes aims to innovate quickly, cost-effectively, and successfully. To ensure this, innovation management control must take on both **operational and strategic tasks** (Schuh et al., 2012). From a strategic perspective, it is about shaping the innovation portfolio with a view to strategic goals and ultimately setting up **"the right" innovation projects**. Operational innovation management control, on the other hand, deals with steering individual innovation projects so that they are "**done right**" in terms of economic efficiency (Landwehr-Zloch, 2022).

Management control includes the coordination of all planning, implementation, and monitoring activities necessary to achieve the project goals in the innovation process, as well as supporting project decisions by providing relevant information (Möller et al., 2016). This specifically means that controllers in innovation projects should take on the following **tasks**:

Overview

- Coordination of the planning and decision-making process for the implementation of innovation activities
- Coordination of sub-goals and plans of the innovation project
- Recording and analysis of specific project targets (costs, payments, deadlines, time-to-use, etc.)
- Evaluation of important process parameters (lead times, process costs, etc.)
- Assessment and cost evaluation of possible alternatives and problem-solving methods
- Regular and timely reporting on the status of the project
- Proposal of measures and preparation of decision templates
- Establishment and maintenance of the project and risk management system
- Audit-proof documentation of project events and project-specific decisions

Important!

Crucial for the success of innovation management control is on the one hand the use of a **standardized process model** and on the other hand the consistent **inclusion of all company functions** involved in the innovation process.

However, it should be ensured that only those actors who can actually contribute to the success of innovation are included in the coordination, as development-specific coordination processes are often time-consuming and can have a negative impact on the time-to-use (Busch et al., 2021a, b). With this in mind, innovation controllers must act as **business partners** and actively support the managers of innovation activities in coordinating the relevant company areas. This requires that appropriate competence profiles for controllers are developed and implemented (Gleich & Munck, 2021).

Example
At Robert Bosch GmbH, a competence model was designed to specifically promote the development of business partner competencies (Nobach & Immel, 2017). ◄

6.2.2 Levels of Management Control of Innovation Activities

Comprehensive management control of innovation activities requires the accomplishment of various coordination and information tasks at **different management levels**, for each of which **specific control aspects** must be considered (Horváth et al., 2020).

Overview
The management control activities can be differentiated according to whether they are carried out at **corporate level**, **multi project level** or individual **project level** (see Fig. 6.1). Specialized innovation controllers can be employed at each level, who must have different skills in order to meet the management control requirements at the individual stages of the innovation process.

Definition

At the **corporate level**, innovation controller must accompany the market-oriented implementation of the innovation strategy, initiate change processes to improve the innovation conditions (resource availability, increased effectiveness in the R&D area, etc.) and support knowledge and change management. At the **multi project level**, it is about advising portfolio management in the selection and compilation of strategically significant innovation projects, highlighting dependencies and synergies between projects as well as analyzing risk potentials. At the **individual project level**, management control primarily aims at the efficiency of project-specific innovation processes (Gleich & Munck, 2021). For this, it is necessary to monitor the project progress in terms of costs, time and quality, manage project risks and identify optimization potentials in project execution.

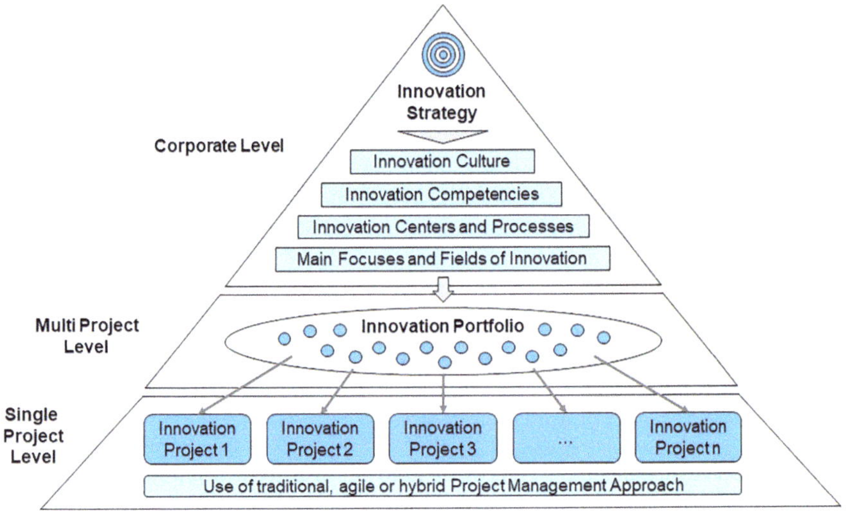

Fig. 6.1 Levels of measuring and controlling innovation activities

In addition to the level model outlined above, **business model approaches** can also be used to structure innovation-specific management control processes. Accordingly, when controlling new business models, it is important to ensure that these are transparently and understandably described (explaining the business), effectively developed (developing the business) and efficiently executed (running the business) (Horváth et al., 2020). Therefore, innovation management control must **establish processes**, that support management in mastering the complexity of business model innovations, ensuring strategic planning and overcoming the challenges in performance measurement and implementation of measures.

Important!
For the **performance management** at the individual management levels, **numerous instruments** are available that **must be sensibly combined and coordinated** to ensure an integrated and consistent management control process.

Overview
At the corporate level, **metrics and metric systems** play a major role in measuring and controlling innovation performance. The selection of the right projects for the innovation portfolio can be made in particular by using **portfolio concepts** as well as **cost and investment calculation methods**.

The performance of individual innovation projects can be controlled by applying various project management control tools (see Fig. 6.2).

6.2.3 *Control Systems to Manage Innovation at Corporate and Portfolio Level*

For a company-wide **innovation management control at corporate level**, a systematics is first necessary to check whether the strategic innovation goals can be realized with the defined search fields, developed ideas and available resources. Both the quantity of ideas and resources as well as their quality must be considered.

Example
If a company wants to develop new functions for existing products for strategic reasons and at the same time generate digital business model innovations, it can analyze with a **holistic management control system** whether both topics can be pursued in parallel and continuously. ◀

A company-wide management control system for innovation activities must also enable the **effectiveness and efficiency of innovation performance** to be

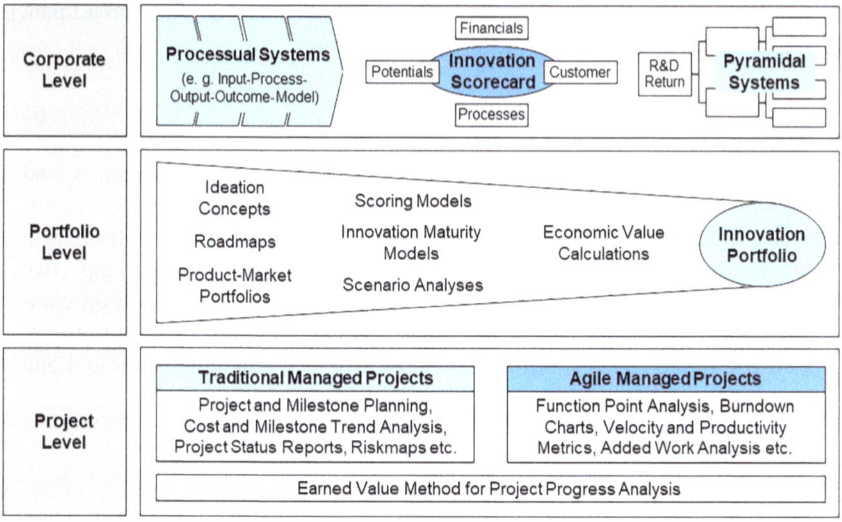

Fig. 6.2 Effective tools to measure and control innovation activities

measured transparently. In addition, it must ensure, that suitable measures are taken to safeguard the success of the innovation processes.

Important!
The primary focus is to assess the **contribution** of innovation activities to the **achievement of strategic objectives and economic success** of the company.

For this purpose, **key performance indicators** are primarily used, which can be sensibly combined and expanded into comprehensive control systems (Fischer et al., 2015). Both quantitative measures (e.g., R&D productivity, number of ideas generated over time, product development time, number of patents) and qualitative indicators (e.g., employee professionalism, degree of elaboration of a product idea, evaluation level of the idea by users or experts) should be applied (for more indicators see, for example, (Kaschny et al., 2015). For the **systematization of indicators** at the company level, procedural and pyramidal approaches as well as the widely used concept of the Balanced Scorecard can be used (see also and in the following (Möller et al., 2016).

Process-oriented concepts, such as the frequently used Input-Process-Output-Outcome Model, consider the performance of innovation along the value creation phases and measure them sequentially using specific indicators that are not mathematically linked. This allows, for example, to analyze how many new products were developed (output) and successfully marketed (outcome) with how many employees in the development area (input), in what time (process). **Pyramidal systems** are based on hierarchically structured business drivers, which are mathematically and logically related to each other and can be condensed into a financial key figure (e.g., R&D return = profit/R&D expense).

Tip
For a holistic innovation management control considering monetary and non-monetary aspects, the concept of the **Balanced Scorecard** is recommended, as it considers the performance of innovation activities from both a financial perspective and a process, potential, and customer perspective (Horváth et al., 2020). An Innovation Balanced Scorecard is based on company-wide formulated innovation goals and can therefore be used not only as a key figure-based control system, but also as a communication tool and to support organizational learning (Fischer et al., 2015).

The design and control of the **project portfolio** for the implementation of the innovation strategy requires a control system that supports the generation and recording of innovation ideas on the one hand, and enables a transparent evaluation and selection of innovation projects on the other. The idea finding can be promoted by incentive systems (e.g., company suggestion system), knowledge databases, and creativity techniques (Kaschny et al., 2015). Uniform project application forms can be used to record and evaluate the generated ideas and project proposals. In this, mandatory criteria should also be defined in order to be able to carry out a first pre-selection. For the evaluation, prioritization, and selection of specific innovation projects, quantitative and **qualitative analysis methods** play a role, as the attractiveness of an innovation depends on both monetary and non-monetary factors (Schuh et al., 2012).

Example

For a differentiated consideration and prioritization of innovation alternatives, **utility analyses** and specific **portfolio concepts** are suitable (see Fig. 6.3). ◄

With **utility analyses**, financial, qualitative, and strategic aspects can be examined, making a holistic assessment of innovation projects possible (Granig, 2007). In addition to defining the evaluation criteria, particular attention should be paid to their weighting. To simplify the evaluation, must-goals can be defined, preference matrices used, and minimum point sums determined (Fiedler, 2020).

Tip

Given the subjectivity in the weighting and evaluation of the target criteria, it is also recommended to **depict various scenarios in the utility analysis**. If the overall evaluation changes only slightly for several scenarios, it can be considered as reliable and used for prioritizing innovation projects (Nobach, 2021).

Scoring Model for Utility Value Analysis

Evaluation Criteria		P1	P2		P3		P4	
Must-Do Project		yes	no		no		no	
Target Criteria	W		S	W*S	S	W*S	S	W*S
Strategic fit	30		2	60	5	150	3	90
Relative Import.			*40%*		*100%*		*60%*	
Degree of Innov.	25		5	125	4	100	1	25
Relative Import.			*100%*		*80%*		*20%*	
Complexity	10		1	10	3	30	4	40
Failure Risk	15		4	60	2	30	3	45
Economic Value	20		2	40	3	60	2	40
∑ Utility Value	100			295		370		240

P1–4 = Projects; W = Weighting; S = Scores (1 Score = Low, 6 Scores = Very Good Target Fulfillment); Relative Import. = Importance compared to the project with highest score

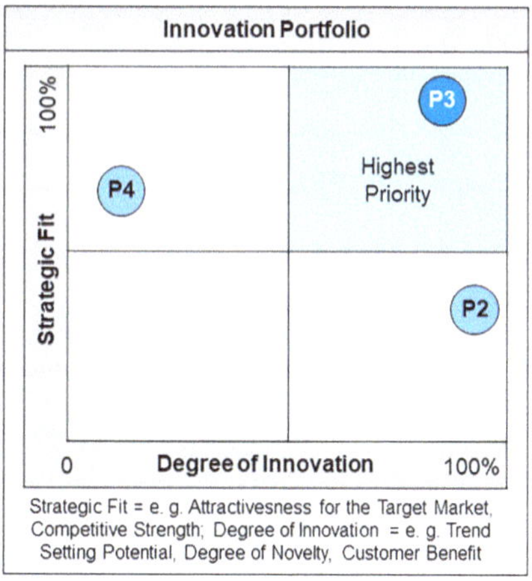

Fig. 6.3 Tools for analyzing the benefit and value of innovation initiatives

For the **visualization** of prioritization results, **portfolio concepts** are suitable (Schuh et al., 2012), which categorize innovation projects, for example, according to their strategic importance and degree of innovation. However, other dimensions, such as technology attractiveness, resource strength, or disruption potential can be chosen for the axes of the portfolio. This makes it possible to prepare decisions about the realization, suspension, or termination of innovation projects in a targeted manner.

The **economic value** of innovation projects can be assessed using static or dynamic investment calculation methods (Granig, 2007).

Background, Additional Information

Static methods, such as cost, profit, and profitability comparisons, are based on average accounting numbers and calculate financing costs only for the average capital employed. In contrast, **dynamic methods** plan the expected cash flows during the project duration and use financial mathematical procedures to represent the project-specific capital interest. The methods often used in business include the internal rate of return method as well as the net present value method and the calculation of the payback period (Landwehr-Zloch, 2022). The **internal rate of return** is usually calculated in the early phases of project evaluation before knowledge of the financing costs and can serve as a benchmark for financing decisions. Once the financing interest rate is known, the **net present value method** can be used to determine the expected value contribution of the innovation project. In business, the so-called Weighted Average Cost of Capital (WACC) is often used as the cost of capital rate (Schmitt, 2013). The WACC represents the weighted average of the company-specific equity and debt interest rates. With the **calculation of the payback period**, the time duration of capital commitment for the project can finally be determined. Since the dynamic investment calculation methods more accurately reflect the capital tied up during the project duration, the use of these methods is preferred for economic evaluation.

Life Cycle Periods	Innovation Phase		Production and Selling Phase				
	2024	2025	2026	2027	2028	2029	2030
Cash Out for R&D Expenditures (USD)	-50.000	-70.000					
Cash In from Sales of New Product (USD)			75.600	78.900	90.240	78.900	70.950
Cash Out for Operating Expenses (USD)			-45.306	-47.340	-54.144	-47.340	-42.570
Free Cash Flow (USD)	-50.000	-70.000	30.294	31.560	36.096	31.560	28.380
Discount Factor (WACC = 6,00%)	0,943	0,890	0,840	0,792	0,747	0,705	0,665
Net Present Value of Free Cash Flow t_{1-5} (USD)	-47.170	-62.300	25.435	24.998	26.973	22.249	18.874
Net Present Value of the Innovation Project (USD)	9.060						
Internal Rate of Return (%)	8,60						
Net Present Value of Free Cash Flow cumulated (USD)	-47.170	-109.470	-84.034	-59.036	-32.063	-9.814	9.060
Pay-Off Time (Interpolation)	7 Years – (9.060 / (9.060 – (-9.814)))					6,52 Years	

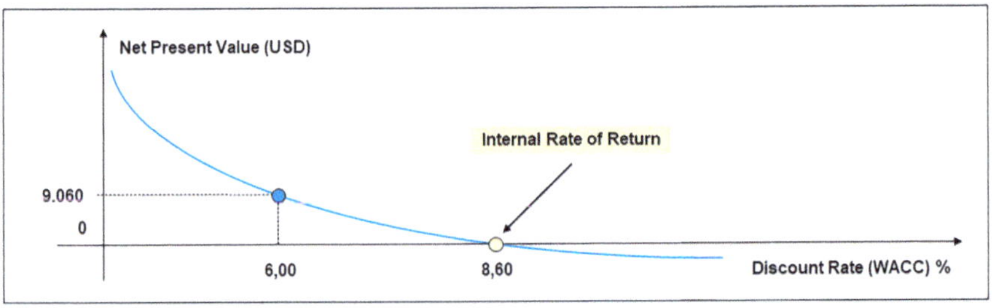

Fig. 6.4 Methods for calculating the economic value of an innovation project

In business, there is often a **parallel use of several investment calculation methods**, to simultaneously represent the project-related value contribution, profitability, and payback period (see Fig. 6.4).

Example
Such a **mix of methods** is used by Airbus and MTU Aero Engines for the business case analysis of development projects (Nobach, 2021). The focus is primarily on analyzing the influence of the planned cash flows and project durations as well as the effects of the cost of capital rate on the project objectives and simulating them from a risk perspective. ◀

For the consideration of innovation risks, **sensitivity analyses, scenario methods, and simulation calculations** can be used (for the use of simulation calculations in risk management control see (Nobach, 2010). Sensitivity analyses are suitable for identifying the particularly critical variables for project evaluation and checking the stability of the project results when varying individual input parameters. With scenario techniques, on the other hand, it can be examined how changes in all input and output factors affect the project-specific target variable (for example, the net present value). The scenario-based approach can also be extended by **Monte Carlo simulations**, which allow a simultaneous variation of all parameters in the evaluation model. Monte Carlo simulations provide a probability distribution of the expected project target figure based on randomly generated samples of the evaluation parameters and can thus provide an additional decision-making basis, especially for innovation projects, for which not all evaluation-relevant figures are known (for example, sales figures for incremental product innovations) (see in detail (Landwehr-Zloch, 2022)).

Important!
Scenario analyses and simulation calculations also play a key role in shaping the innovation portfolio, as the calculation results form the basis for the **creation of risk classes** and the definition of target values (hurdle rates) for project selection. The categorization of risks then allows the construction of an evaluation matrix for comparing risk and attractiveness of individual innovation projects (Schreckeneder, 2013).

Tip
With regard to the composition of the innovation portfolio, an **assessment of potential project dependencies** should also be carried out, as innovation

projects can influence each other in practice (for example, due to conceptual dependencies). Here, the availability of resources and know-how must also be considered in order to achieve a sensible prioritization of individual projects. In this context, it is particularly important to ensure that not too many projects are running simultaneously, as this can lead to staff overload and bottlenecks in key positions. Therefore, it is often recommended to **work on projects sequentially rather than in parallel**. Moreover, limiting the allocable budget volume for certain projects can be an effective tool to ensure a balanced composition of the project portfolio (Fiedler, 2020).

6.2.4 Requirements for Managing Innovation Activities at Project Level

For a meaningful design and application of management control instruments at the individual project level, the **peculiarities of innovation projects** must first be considered. These result, on the one hand, from the fact that the outcome of such projects is usually uncertain and, on the other hand, from the temporal discrepancy between costs and revenues. Therefore, instruments are required that enable a systematic approach to the planning, control and management of innovation activities. In addition, the use of instruments must be based on the type of innovation and the degree of innovation and consider the requirements in the individual phases of the innovation process (Fischer et al., 2015).

Important!
Furthermore, when choosing methods of management control, it must be checked whether the **project management is traditional, agile** or follows a **hybrid approach**.

While **traditionally managed projects** can rely on detailed planning concepts (project structure plan, process plan, time and cost plan, etc.), target-actual comparisons, milestone analyses, and trend diagrams, **agile work methods** require instruments that support flexible resource allocation, open information exchange, and constructive discourse while simultaneously allowing continuous review of project progress. In business, innovation processes that have so far been structured according to traditional approaches are increasingly supplemented with agile elements (Ulrich & Rieg, 2020), for example, by working traditionally in some phases and according to agile principles in other stages (Landwehr-Zloch, 2022). For instance, the banking group BNP Paribas uses a combination of agile and traditional approaches in so-called "**agile mixed**" **projects** when developing customer-specific software solutions (Nobach, 2021).

In the following, we will first introduce management control tools for traditionally managed innovation projects, and then present methods for agile managed projects.

6.2.5 Management Control Tools for Traditionally Managed Innovation Projects

In traditional management, innovation projects are usually divided into **sequential phases**. The partial results of the individual project phases generally build on each other and ultimately lead to a previously specified overall project result. Therefore, after the project definition phase, the structure and course of the innovation project must first be planned in detail (for example, according to the waterfall or V-model).

Overview
Traditional project management control requires different **planning tools**, to be able to comprehensively define and monitor the innovation activities with regard to cost, quality, and time (see Fig. 6.5).

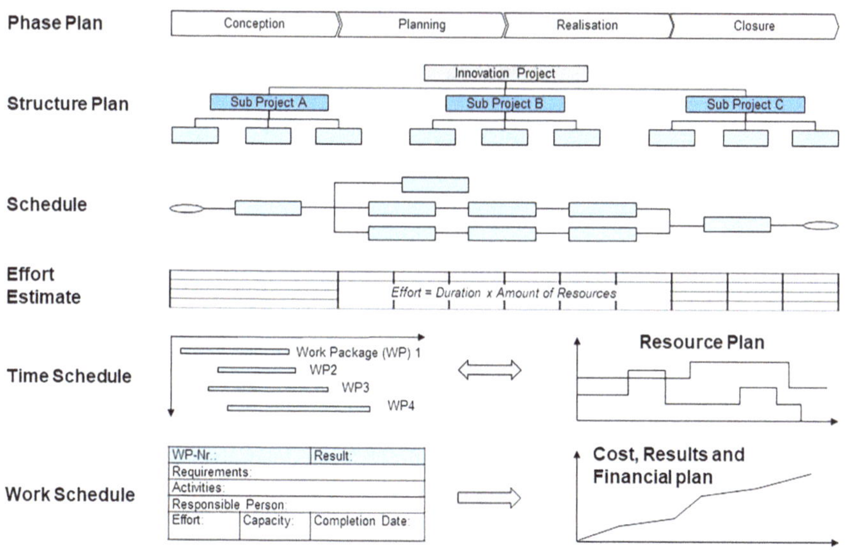

Fig. 6.5 Basic elements of traditional project planning

The planning activities begin with the creation of a **phase plan**, in which the success factors for the individual project sections are specifically represented. Following this, a **project structure plan** is designed, which includes all work packages and milestones necessary for achieving the innovation goals. After defining the structure, the sequence and interfaces of the defined work packages must be determined in a **process plan (activity schedule)**.

The next step is to estimate the effort for each work package. The initial **effort estimation** plays a central role in innovation management control, as the accuracy of the estimate often determines project success in business. The predicted effort determines the resource requirements for schedule-driven planning and the processing time of the project for resource-driven planning. In the **schedule planning**, the duration of the individual work packages is determined and recorded in a task list. From the time planning, the **resource planning** can be derived. This aims to ensure the availability of the necessary capacities for the innovation activities.

After completing the resource planning, **detailed work plans** should be created for each work package. The work plans contain all necessary innovation activities as well as those responsible for their implementation and thus form the basis for cost, result, and financial planning. In the **cost planning**, all directly attributable costs for the work packages must first be determined and the overhead costs for the development and construction personnel allocated. In addition, risk surcharges (contingencies) and financing costs must be included in the planning.

Based on the forecast of costs and results, a detailed **financial plan** must be prepared, on order to predict the project-specific cash inflows and outflows, identify possible liquidity bottlenecks, and initiate suitable financing measures (see in detail (Zirkler et al., 2019)).

Tip

As part of the creation of the sub-plans, the expected **project risks** should also be analyzed in detail and appropriate control measures initiated (Granig, 2007). Numerous methods and tools are available for this, which can be differentiated according to whether they are used for the identification, evaluation, documentation, or control of risks.

For **risk identification**, checklists, error trees, or scenario analyses can be used, which must be aligned with the framework conditions and individual stakeholder interests of the innovation project. Different methods should be combined and risks differentiated according to project phases to ensure a holistic risk management (Nobach, 2021).

The **evaluation of risks** can be done with qualitative or quantitative approaches. For each risk, not only the probability of occurrence and potential damage but also its change over the course of the project must be estimated (Kuster et al., 2022). Moreover, it is useful to categorize the identified **threats** (for example, into acceptable versus existential risks, event and planning risks) and **differentiate them by size classes**.

For the **management of risks**, passive and active strategies (for example, risk acceptance or initiation of mitigation measures) as well as key performance indicators can be used (Nobach, 2010). For the documentation and reporting of project risks, **Risk Inventories and Risk Maps** are suitable (see Fig. 6.6) or also specific risk cockpits (Bär et al., 2017).

In the **project implementation phase**, primarily tools are needed that enable effective project progress control and risk management as well as transparent project reporting. Here, particular attention must be paid to the appropriate preparation of project-related information (Schreckeneder, 2013), as these are used for different purposes of project management (for example, for internal project resource control or for reporting to the project steering committee).

Important!
For the generation of these data, the **project information system** must be designed in such a way that it can be checked at any time whether the innovation-specific target sizes **budget, time, and quality** are still within the given framework. In addition, tools are needed to analyze the risks and monitor the status of the implementation of measures.

For the monitoring of deadlines and budgets, **Milestone and Cost Trend Diagrams** can be applied (see Fig. 6.7).

The **Milestone Trend Analysis** shows, unlike a simple bar chart, whether delays are to be expected in an innovation project for individual stages, work packages or

Basic Structure of a Risk Inventory

No.	Risk	Cause	Likelihood	Impact	...
1					
2					
3					
...					

...	Project Phase	Measure	Status	Respon-sible	...
1					
2					
3					
...					

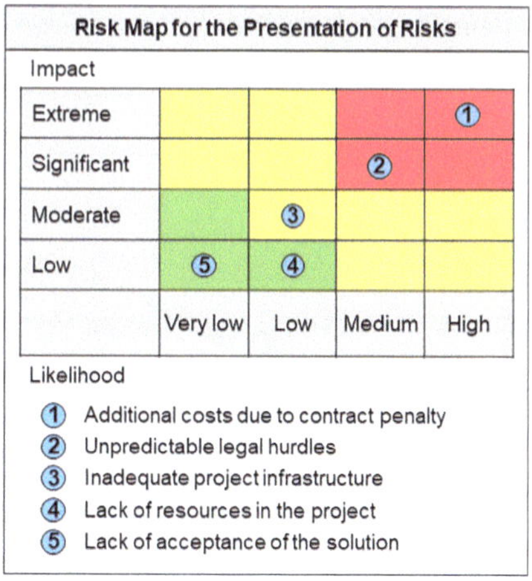

Fig. 6.6 Documentation and reporting tools for innovation risks

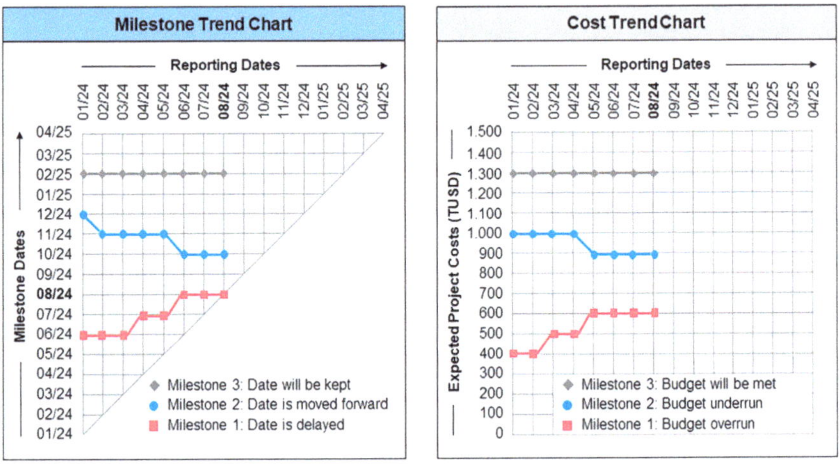

Fig. 6.7 Examples of a Milestone and Cost Trend Analysis

milestones. A continuously rising curve indicates that planning may be too optimistic, while a falling curve may be an indication that the time buffers planned are too high. A fluctuating curve can mean that the planning is subject to a high degree of uncertainty (Zirkler et al., 2019).

Cost Trend Charts can be used to clearly illustrate how the expected costs for individual work packages change during the course of the project (Noé, 2017).

Cost data can also be combined with time-related information and depicted in a **Time/Cost Trend Diagram** (see Fig. 6.8), to track budget consumption over time (Fiedler, 2020).

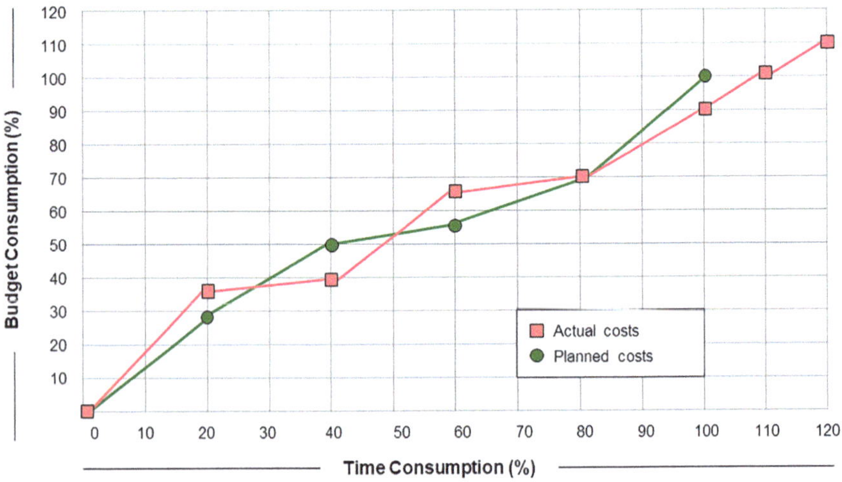

Fig. 6.8 Example of a Time/Cost Trend Diagram

When using such time/cost trend charts, however, it should be noted that a project can be behind schedule and/or exceed the cost budget even if there is no deviation of actual costs from planned costs at the time of observation and the cost consumption matches the time consumption. This is the case when the **progress of performance** does not correspond to the cost and time consumption and more project work hast to be done than time and budget are available.

Tip
With this in mind, a control system should be established that allows for the **continuous monitoring of the completion status** of the projects (Kuster et al., 2022).

The **degree of completion** of innovation projects can be measured using input- and output-oriented methods. The input-related methods include the Efforts-Expended method and the widely used **Cost-to-Cost method** (Fiedler, 2020). These methods determine the project-specific degree of completion based on the relation of actual effort (for example, measured in person-days) or actual costs to the projected effort or cost volume for the entire project. For an output-based determination of progress, the milestone method or the 0/50/100 method can be used. According to the milestone method, the degree of completion is derived from the ratio of achieved milestones to the milestones planned for the entire project. The 0/50/100 method, on the other hand, assesses project progress based on work packages (Dechange, 2020). Accordingly, the degree of completion for completed work packages is 100%, for started packages 50% and for packages not yet started 0%. To ensure a comparable measurement of the progress of innovation projects, the approach to determining the degree of completion should be uniformly specified in a **Earning Rule** across the company (Nobach, 2021).

The determination of the project-specific degree of completion also plays a central role in the application of the so-called **Earned Value Method**.

Important!
The **Earned Value Method** enables **integrated cost and performance control**, as it analyzes the Earned Value of the project based on a simultaneous consideration of costs, times and progress of performance.

The **Earned Value (EV)** is understood as **planned costs of the achieved performance** (= planned costs of the actual project progress) and compared with the accumulated actual costs (AC) and the cumulative planned costs (PC) for the project (Zirkler et al., 2019).

If the Earned Value is above or below the actual costs, the **Cost Variance** indicates an unforeseen resource consumption. If the Earned Value deviates from the planned costs, this indicates a **Schedule Variance** in the sense of non-scheduled work progress.

Example

For a long-term innovation project with several work packages, the Earned Value Method can provide a **transparent presentation of the project progress** (see Fig. 6.9).

In the example in Fig. 6.9, the negative Cost Variance in August (EV 13,500 T€ − AC 18,250 T€ = −4750 T€) signals that the budget has been exceeded. In addition, the project is behind schedule, as the Schedule Variance also takes a negative value (EV 13,500 T€ − PV 16,000 T€ = −2500 T€). ◀

Background, Additional Information

The Earned Value Concept also provides specific efficiency indicators that can be used to forecast the total costs and completion duration of projects (Menze, 2013). The cost efficiency (Cost Performance Index) results from the ratio of the Earned Value to the actual costs and indicates whether the costs have been exceeded (value < 1) or undercut (value > 1). For the project considered above, the value in August is 0.74 (= EV 13,500 T€/AC 18,250 T€). If the cost efficiency is related to the project cost budget (BUD), the expected total costs can be determined, assuming that the remaining work will continue to be carried out with the same efficiency (Fiedler, 2020). For the project considered, total costs of 33,796 T€

Initial Project Data: Project Duration: January – December 2024, Total Cost Budget (BUD) = 25.000 TUSD

Project Status 8/2024	Jan	Feb	Mar	Apr	May	Jun	Jul	Aug	Sep	Oct	Nov	Dec	Total
Work Package 1	1.000	1.000	2.000	2.000									6.000
Work Package 2					2.000	2.000	3.000	3.000	2.500	2.500			15.000
Work Package 3											2.000	2.000	4.000
Planned Value cumulated (TUSD	**1.000**	**2.000**	**4.000**	**6.000**	**8.000**	**10.000**	**13.000**	**16.000**	**18.500**	**21.000**	**23.000**	**25.000**	**25.000**
Work Package 1*	10.0	25.0	80.0	90.0	100.0	100.0	100.0	**100,0**					100,0
Work Package 2*	0.0	0.0	0.0	5.0	15.0	25.0	40.0	**50,0**	= 6.000 / 25.000 + 15.000 / 25.000 / 2				50,0
Work Package 3													0,0
Percentage of Completion (%)	**2,4**	**6,0**	**19,2**	**24,6**	**33,0**	**39,0**	**48,0**	**54,0**					54,0
Earned Value cumulated (TUSD)	**600**	**1.500**	**4.800**	**6.150**	**8.250**	**9.750**	**12.000**	**13.500**	= 0,54 x 25.000				13.500
Work Package 1	750	1.250	2.250	1.250	250								5.750
Work Package 2				1.500	2.000	2.500	3.500	3.000					12.500
Work Package 3													0
Actual Costs culmulated (TUSD)	**750**	**2.000**	**4.250**	**7.000**	**9.250**	**11.750**	**15.250**	**18.250**					18.250

* Based on report from project manager on evaluation date

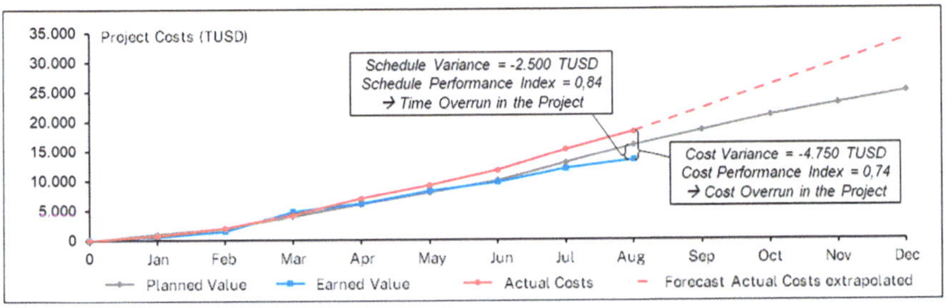

Fig. 6.9 Calculation example for an Earned Value Analysis

(= BUD 25,000 T€/0.74) are therefore to be expected. The time efficiency (Schedule Performance Index) expresses the ratio of the Earned Value to the planned costs and informs whether the project is behind schedule (value < 1) or ahead of schedule (value > 1). In the project example, the value for August is 0.84 (= EV 13,500 T€/PV 16,000 T€). If the originally planned project duration is divided by the time efficiency, the forecast total duration for the innovation project is obtained (Dechange, 2020). Therefore, for the project considered above, a total duration of 14.2 months (= 12 months/0.84) is expected, assuming a constant time efficiency.

Important!
An effective innovation management control must not only continuously monitor the project progress, but also actively manage the project risks. This requires a **well-developed risk management system** to track the risks identified before the start of the project, analyze newly emerging risks and monitor the implementation of risk measures (Bär et al., 2017).

For this purpose, a detailed **Risk List** is suitable. In addition to the information from the Risk Inventory, this list should also contain deadlines for reviewing risks and measures as well as a prioritization of risks. The ranking of risks can be created using risk priority numbers (for qualitative evaluation) or mathematical expected values (for quantitative evaluation) (Dechange, 2020).

Based on this, the particularly critical risks (for example, the top 5 or 10 risks) can be selected and regularly reported in the project steering committee using a **Risk Map**. In addition, at the project management level, a **routine meeting** should take place weekly or biweekly, in which the remaining risks and the implementation of measures are also reviewed. In addition, **risk analysis workshops** can be conducted at certain intervals to discuss the risk situation and development in detail with the project team.

For this purpose, **checklists and catalogs of measures** for specific innovation risks are suitable (Kraus & Westermann, 2019). In this context, communication measures should also be considered, as they are often the most effective actions of risk management (for the fundamental importance of communication in the innovation process see Chap. 5).

The project information generated with the various planning and analysis methods must finally be presented with suitable **reporting tools** at different levels (for example, in the project jour fixe, steering committee, or project audit). In addition to ad-hoc reports, **standard reports** should also be created regularly to continuously and comparably inform about the project progress.

The reporting for innovation projects should be designed in such a way that it best meets the specific information needs of the various report recipients or users. This can be achieved, for example, through **traffic light views** or **individualized analysis options**. Moreover, the reports should contain meaningful comments and recommendations and point out decision-making needs specific to innovation.

Important!
In this context, special attention must also be paid to ensuring that **developments and figures that appear unrealistic are not ignored**, but rather taken seriously and validated. Otherwise, serious mistakes can be made in the project (Madauss, 2020).

Example
Structured **Status Reports** and **Dashboards** can be used for transparent project reporting (see Fig. 6.10). ◀

The reporting system for innovation projects must be both quality-assured and as efficient as possible. The **opportunities of digitalization** offer essential starting points for this. With the help of modern access technologies (for example, in-memory technology) and more powerful tools for data integration and analysis (Business Analytics), project-specific information can be analyzed more quickly and in depth. In addition, standard reports for innovation projects can be fully automated and created in a short time at very low cost using Robotic Process Automation (RPA) (Nobach, 2019).

The use of standardized and transparent reports is not only a key success factor in the traditional management of innovation projects, but also for the performance measurement of **agile managed innovation activities**. This also applies to the use

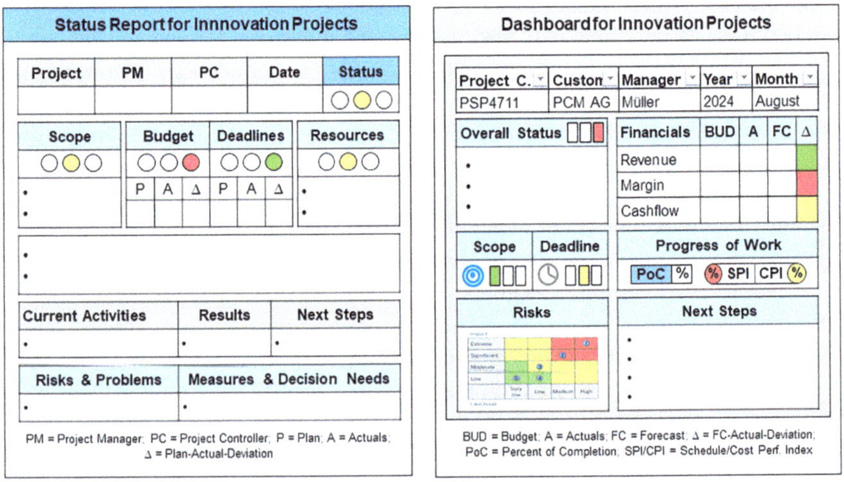

Fig. 6.10 Examples of report formats in project reporting

of planning and analysis tools, as even with agile work, project goals and activities must be planned, monitored and controlled. However, the planning, control and reporting system must be designed differently to meet the requirements of agility.

6.2.6 Management Control Tools for Agile Managed Innovation Projects

Background, Additional Information
Agile project management is used in the context of innovation processes, particularly for development projects for which the requirements and objectives can only be roughly outlined at the start of the project (for example, in the field of software development). However, many **companies are increasingly relying on agile working methods** for other innovation projects in order to better respond to rapid market changes and higher levels of complexity (Wobser, 2022).

The use of agile working methods is necessary, among other reasons, because today it is often not just new products or innovative services that need to be developed, but also the corresponding **business models and marketing concepts**. Such projects require a high degree of flexibility and adaptability from the innovation teams in order to be able to react dynamically to changes in content, timing, and finances.

Background, Additional Information
Agile working techniques follow the principle of **System Thinking**, which aims to solve complex problems that cannot be solved by linear thinking patterns (Böhm, 2019). The most well-known approaches include KANBAN and SCRUM (Schastok et al., 2018). Given the high prevalence of **SCRUM** (Ulrich & Rieg, 2020), the following explanations focus on management control tools for projects that are processed according to this approach.

The SCRUM approach assumes that the outcome of a project cannot be planned in detail from the outset, but rather **iteratively and incrementally** in short time intervals (Sprints); (see fundamentally (Schwaber & Sutherland, 2020). Therefore, project management control can usually only rely on a rough cost and schedule planning for the overall project (Schopka, 2015). This leads to the fact that detailed target-actual comparisons in the classical sense are no longer possible.

Important!
Therefore, **management control must continuously monitor the progress of work in the sprints**, to ensure that the work results are reliably delivered with predictable quality.

The **planning accuracy** for the delivery dates and results is usually higher due to the agile approach than with a classical approach. Forecasts reaching further into the future (more than three sprints) are less accurate in scope, but exact in timing (Böhm, 2019).

Important!
With this in mind, the **ongoing planning of project activities** in agile innovation projects is of central importance.

According to the SCRUM concept, planning takes place before each sprint to define the sprint goal and the tasks to be completed and to estimate the effort for the project activities. This approach requires not only a flexible allocation of innovation resources but also a suitable **planning methodology**, to be able to predict the project-specific implementation efforts as accurately as possible (Nobach, 2021).

For this purpose, the **Function Point Method** is suitable, for example, which is often used in innovative digitization projects in practice (Schmid, 2019). Based on experience from previous development projects, the expected efforts for new innovation projects can be determined. To do this, one first analyzes the activities carried out in past projects or work packages to realize system functions or user stories and evaluates these with points that express the **implementation complexity and other effort drivers** (Fiedler, 2020).

Subsequently, for each Function/Story Point, the work effort incurred is determined and statistically a **Function Point Curve** is calculated (see Fig. 6.11). For upcoming innovation activities, the Function Points can now be determined and the expected effort can be read off the curve.

The effort estimation for the individual sprints is carried out by the agile innovation teams themselves. The remaining project effort is monitored daily together

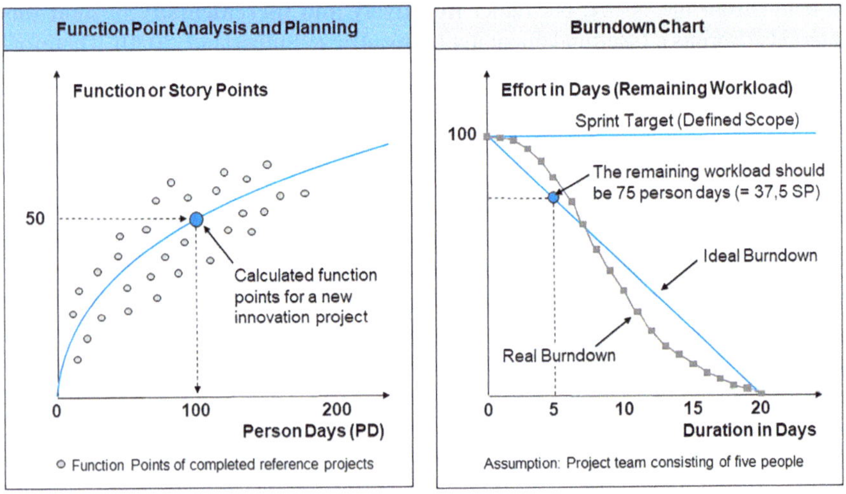

Fig. 6.11 Example of a Function Point Curve and a Burndown Chart

with the project progress during the **implementation phase**. For this purpose, a **Burndown Chart** can be used (Friedl et al., 2022), which shows how much work was planned for a sprint and what is actually still to be done (see Fig. 6.11).

The **ideal burndown** (linear connection between the two axes) indicates the daily work effort required to achieve the sprint goal (target) (Dechange, 2020). The **actual burndown** represents the remaining effort at the end of each sprint day. For the evaluation of planned and actual effort, person-days or story points can be used, which are determined by the sprint team depending on the complexity, quantity, and uncertainty of the tasks. A story point often corresponds to one to two person-days (Fiedler, 2020).

The Burndown Chart is a crucial tool for monitoring the progress of individual sprints, as the planned work scope is usually fixed at the sprint level. However, there may be **changes to the scope for the overall project** during the project term, which are not reflected in the Burndown Chart. For a cross-sprint view of the overall project progress, a **Burnup Chart** should be used, as it can also represent changes in the project scope (see Fig. 6.12).

Example

The Burnup Chart above (see Fig. 6.12) shows the planned project scope and the current project progress in a transparent manner. The basic idea corresponds to that of the Burndown Chart, but the curve is rising, so that scope changes in the course of the project become visible (Möller, 2020). Burnup Charts are therefore particularly **suitable for overall project control at the management level**. If the already described Earned Value Method is also used for this purpose, meaningful control information for management can be generated (Fiedler, 2020). ◄

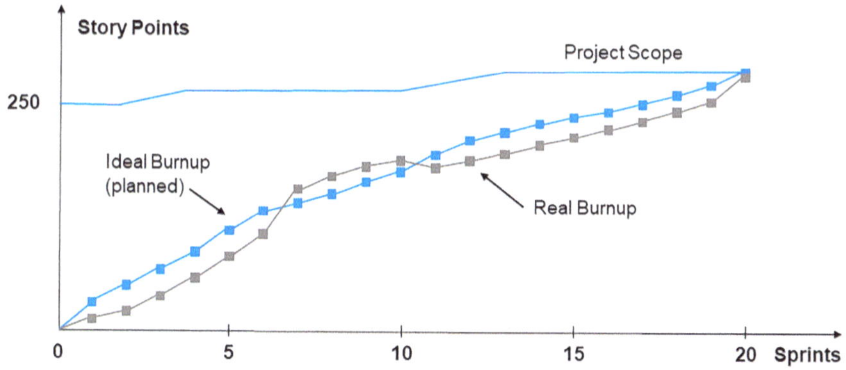

Fig. 6.12 Example of a Burnup Chart to control the overall project progress

In addition to the methods presented for effort estimation and visualization of project progress, **specific metrics** can be used to effectively manage agile innovation projects (see Fig. 6.13).

When using these metrics, a distinction must also be made between the internal view of the sprint teams (delivery) and the external perspective of management or stakeholders (product owner). **Internal metrics** help sprint teams monitor development and delivery activities. **External metrics**, on the other hand, are intended to help management control cost and result situations and maintain an overview of resources, deadlines, quality, and effectiveness.

Important!
For the management control of the **sprint performance**, the **sprint velocity** is particularly important, as this metric can predict the workload that the innovation team can handle in a sprint (Böhm, 2019).

Velocity measures the amount of work completed in a sprint (usually reported with story points) and is typically not constant throughout the project (Kuster et al., 2022). Therefore, the **average velocity** of the last three to five sprints should be used for sprint planning. If the processing speed deviates significantly from the previous average over time, this may be an indication that the team is currently in a high or low phase. An increasing or decreasing velocity can also be due to a change in team capacity (Wanner, 2018).

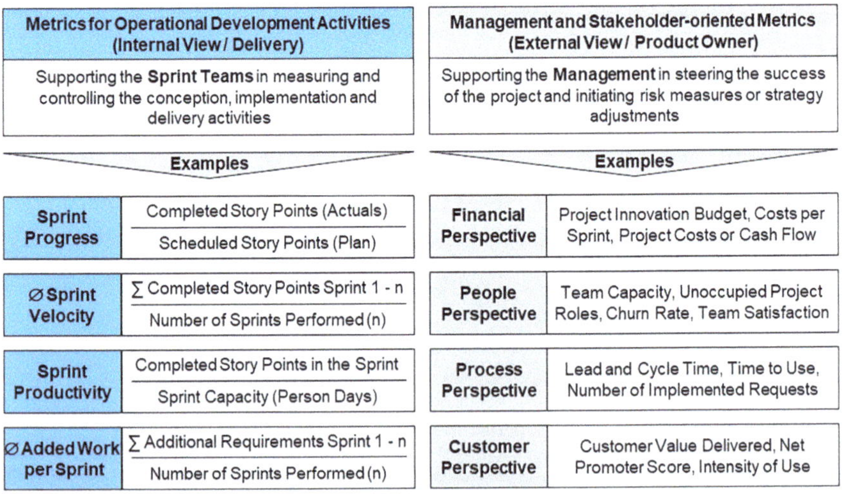

Fig. 6.13 Specific metrics to control agile managed innovation projects

Therefore, it is advisable to measure the **sprint productivity** in addition to the velocity. This metric, also known as the "focus factor," relates the targeted or completed workload of a sprint to the planned or actual team capacity. Like velocity, this metric should increase and stabilize after the first sprints, as it is expected that innovation teams will work more focused over time when using agile methods. Sprint productivity can also be used to compare the performance of individual teams (Prowareness, 2014). However, it should always be considered whether and to what extent changes (additional user stories) have occurred in the sprint.

To measure the unplanned scope increase during the project, the **added work** metric is suitable, which shows how much new requirements are added on average in each sprint.

In addition to the metrics explained, other agile metrics can be used, for example, to measure estimation accuracy (= Estimated effort/actual effort) or reliability (= planned story points/completed story points) of innovation teams (see for example (Sellinger et al., 2020)).

Overview
From the **perspective of management** and stakeholders, a set of key performance indicators is required, that enables management control of the entire innovation project across all sprints. The individual metrics should be selected in such a way that they provide information on both the financial situation of the project and non-financial success factors. In this regard, it is advisable to determine the indicators according to the already mentioned concept of the **Balanced Scorecard** (Möller et al., 2016).

From the **financial perspective**, for example, the degree of budget compliance, the cost per sprint or the project-related return on investment (= completed story points or user stories/investment costs) are suitable as control metrics. For the **potential perspective**, non-monetary indicators such as team capacity, turnover rate or satisfaction of project team members are important. To measure the project goals pursued from a **process perspective**, time variables such as time-to-use and efficiency indicators (for example, effort expended/available development time) and quality indicators (for example, number of errors occurred during product tests) can be used. For the **customer perspective**, the Value Delivered (= customer benefit of a implemented requirement evaluated in points) or the Net Promoter Score (customer recommendation rate) can be used as agile metrics.

Important!
Management control of agile innovation projects must not only focus on measuring the achievement of project goals, but must also actively support the **management of project risks** (see in detail (Brandstäter, 2013)).

This requires an effective and adaptable risk management concept, as the environment and working methods in agile innovation projects are regularly characterized by high dynamics. In agile project management, the **early detection of errors (fail fast)** is an integral part, so the systematic identification of risks is of central importance (Böhm, 2019). For this, the Sprint Planning and the Task Board play a crucial role.

In **Sprint Planning**, the requirements should be consistently broken down into tasks and mapped in an implementation path. The plan should be designed from a risk perspective so that the most difficult tasks are tackled first (Kuster et al., 2022). During the sprint, the **Task Board** is an important tool for early risk detection. By providing a detailed description of the activities and careful recording of work progress, maximum transparency about performance risks can be created (Nobach, 2021).

In addition, a project-specific **Risk List** should be maintained to track the identified risks and the measures initiated for them (Kusay-Merkle, 2021). Due to the self-organization in the context of agile work, special attention should be paid to social and quality-related risks. Communicative measures are particularly suitable for coping with social risks. To limit quality risks, clear criteria must be defined as to when a work package is considered completed from a quality perspective (Definition of Done). Moreover, the **"Inspect and Adapt" Principle** of agile working methods is an effective approach to reduce potential risks by quickly adapting the result requirements (Dechange, 2020).

The risks must finally be reported transparently along with the project progress and other success-critical factors both within the team and to the project management and stakeholders. This requires a **project reporting** that is both aligned with the requirements of agile working methods and best satisfies the information needs of management and stakeholders.

For the **reporting in the innovation teams**, the **Task Board** is particularly important because it shows the sprint backlog and provides an overview of all user stories and tasks as well as their respective work progress (Kusay-Merkle, 2021). In addition, key figures and diagrams can be integrated to support the innovation team in monitoring the sprint activities. Furthermore, innovation management control can provide additional reports such as a Theme Park for internal team reporting. With this report, also known as a **Parking Lot Diagram**, the stage of completion of individual product functions or modules of an innovation project can be clearly presented (Wanner, 2018). Reports for managing agile innovation teams should be as flexible and not too detailed as possible, since rigid report structures are not compatible with an agile way of working (Dufft et al., 2018).

For **reporting at the management level**, standard reports and Dashboards, as in traditional project management, are particularly suitable. In agile innovation projects, however, these often need to be more differentiated due to the greater involvement of clients and stakeholders in order to satisfy different information needs. This also involves presenting **conflicts of objectives** between stakeholders or scenarios for identifiable side effects of the project, which can occur, for example, in digitization projects (Schmid, 2019). Reporting for agile innovation projects must ultimately be designed in such a way that it enables **open information exchange** as well as quick, goal-oriented decisions and promotes collective learning. The experiences and results from the project work should also be documented as "Lessons Learned" in knowledge databases. In this context, it is also important to ensure that the **intellectual property** of the innovation performance is comprehensively protected. How this can be achieved will be demonstrated in the following chapter.

6.3 Securing Intellectual Property

It is becoming increasingly clear that companies in times of global economic dynamics must shift from a rather cautious adoption of new developments to independent sources of ideas and their systematic use. This means that **improving their innovation capability is indispensable** (Busch, 2003a).

The **strategic planning of innovations**, their development, and their realization on the market are a crucial element in corporate management.

The comprehensive protection of intellectual property required for this is characterized by the term "**IP management**" (intellectual property) (Reich, 2021; Wurzer et al., 2016).

The main aspects of IP management include:

- the identification of innovative problems, derived from the comprehensive global development of various policy fields, the market, the economy, science, literature, and patent activities,
- the acquisition of the necessary innovation competencies and the Basic knowledge of patent law among relevant employees, as well as the motivation of all company employees,
- the development and further development of an innovation-friendly infrastructure within the company, with its informal, material, personnel, and financial prerequisites,
- the creation and continuous updating of a portfolio of protective rights, and
- the protection of one's own intellectual property rights and the defense against infringements of others' rights.

The types of innovations that are most urgent for each company and how to secure them legally depends, among other things, on the position of the company's products or services in the product life cycle and on the specific and foreseeable market situation.

Based on the market growth-market share matrix explained in Sect. 2.3, the development of a protective rights strategy can be based on the following **portfolio** (see Fig. 6.14).

If companies are at the beginning of the introduction phase in the **product life cycle** with their most important products—as is currently typical for many companies in technology and start-up centers—completely new requirements for

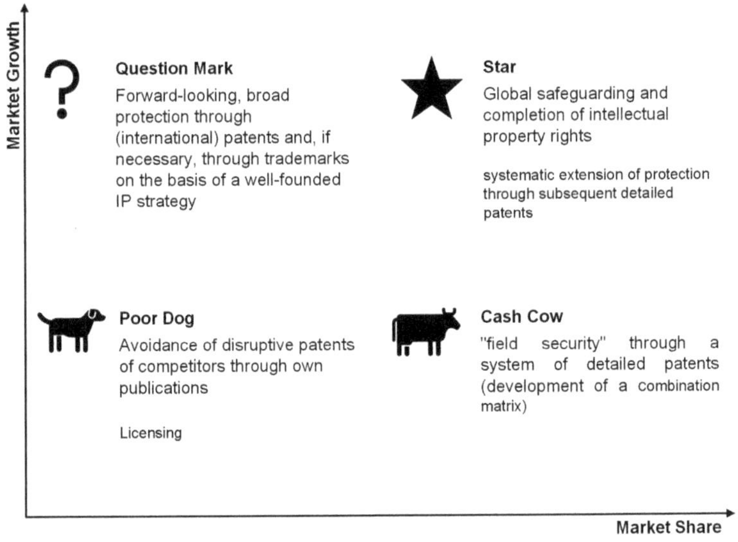

Fig. 6.14 Protective rights strategies depending on the level of invention and market development

personnel and organizational development suddenly arise when transitioning from prototype to market (see Fig. 6.15).

Product development must now give priority to the establishment of manufacturing and marketing processes. Process and organizational innovations, as well as continuous improvement processes, come more into the focus of innovation management. A forward-looking broad protection through (international) patents and possibly trademarks based on a solid protective rights strategy becomes indispensable.

There is also a significant need for technical and middle-level personnel, especially for manufacturing, marketing, and maintenance.

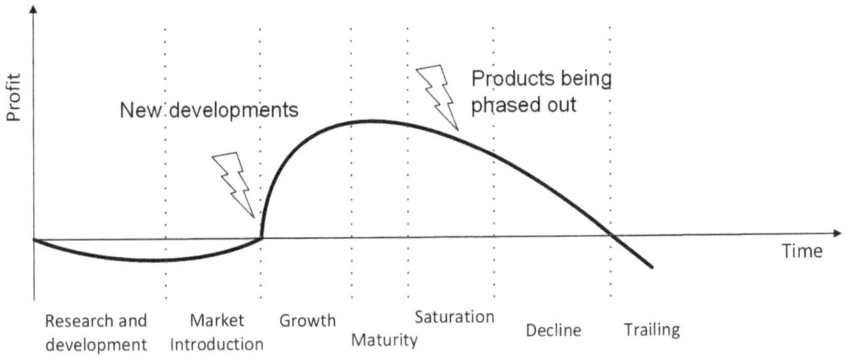

Fig. 6.15 Product Lifecycle

If a company's products or services are essentially in the saturation or even decline phase, product and service innovations must be urgently initiated, supported by a system of detailed patents (based on a combination matrix, see Fig. 2.4: Portfolio matrix in Sect. 2.1).

It is desirable to achieve as even a distribution as possible of products and product groups across the individual phases of the product life cycle.

Innovation and protective rights strategies are inseparably linked with training and further education strategies and the establishment of corresponding learning infrastructures (Vahs & Burmeister, 2005).

It is advantageous if the protection of intellectual property can rely on a suitable **infrastructure**. Depending on the business areas, size, structure, and legal form of the companies, as well as the corporate culture, there may be a multi-layered structure for the development of innovations.

The **first level**—the basis—of IP rights work lies at the broad level of the **employees** of the company.

Individual employees should have the motivation and competence to recognize problems in the work objects, the work tools, and the work organization, to develop ideas for their solution, to forward these ideas within the company structures, and to participate in their realization.

The effectiveness of developing improvement suggestions can be made more effective by involving several employees in **creative groups** (improvement activists, improvement teams, innovator collectives).

It is recommended that those involved in research and development have a basic training in the field of protective rights work.

The **second level** can be formed by **patent engineers** with corresponding competencies.

The patent engineers guide the employees towards strategic protective rights goals and advise on existing creative ideas. They conduct literature and patent searches to protect the ideas and monitor the intellectual property activities of competitors in the market.

The consulting activities of patent engineers typically focus on their own company.

Generally, a degree in engineering or natural sciences is required for training as a patent engineer.

In the collaboration between patent engineers and inventive employees, the following questions should be particularly considered:

- Who identified and named the problem?
- Who had the inventive idea for solving the problem?
- Were individuals from other companies (customers, suppliers, …) involved in the idea generation?
- Has the inventive idea been kept secret so far?
- Does the idea concern a product, a process, or an organizational solution?
- Has the idea been documented in writing or visually represented?
- How should the significance of the idea be assessed? Can the significance be represented in an idea matrix (invention matrix)?

Larger and research-intensive companies or institutes may—as a **third level**—have their own patent attorneys who, in collaboration with the patent engineers, handle the following tasks:

- Patent searches
- Patent applications and patent monitoring
- Trademark protection
- Design protection
- Licensing law & contract design
- Pre-litigation intellectual property disputes
- Proceedings before authorities and courts

Patent engineers serve as a bridge between inventors or innovators and patent attorneys.

6.4 Appropriate Preparation of the Invention for Transfer

6.4.1 Testing of Functional Models

Before the design of a new or further development reaches the market through approvals and markings, it is almost always advisable to have a sample or a functional model available to test the functionality, the essential parameters of the objective, and possibly also the technology of production.

Companies can have their own model construction or a development laboratory for this purpose—or they can assign tasks to specialized firms.

For developments that are to be transferred from scientific institutes to industry, "Scientific Instrumentation" facilities serve as a bridge. Such facilities can either be integrated into the research institutions themselves—or they are closely connected to the research institutions as independent companies. An effective transfer of research results into practical implementation is a key characteristic of an innovation-friendly infrastructure in a region.

Precision engineering—including hardware and software development—can play a significant role in the transfer of scientific results into innovative products (Busch, 2009; Busch & Busch, 2015).

6.4.2 Product Approval

Clinical Approval

Special guidelines apply specifically to medical products that must be complied with before the products can be brought to market. The EU regulation of April 5, 2017, for medical products states:

"(1) The EU legal framework for medical devices—excluding in-vitro diagnostics—consists of Council Directive 90/385/EEC and Council Directive 93/42/EEC. However, to create a robust, transparent, predictable, and sustainable legal framework for medical devices that ensures a high level of safety and health protection while also promoting innovation, a fundamental revision of these directives is necessary.

(2) Based on a high level of health protection for patients and users, this regulation aims to ensure a smoothly functioning internal market for medical devices, taking into account small and medium-sized enterprises active in this sector. In addition, this regulation sets high standards for the quality and safety of medical devices, which should alleviate general safety concerns regarding these products. Both objectives are pursued in parallel; they are inseparably linked and absolutely equal in rank. Based on Article 114 of the Treaty on the Functioning of the European Union (TFEU), this regulation harmonizes the legal provisions for the marketing and commissioning of medical devices and their accessories on the Union market, which can thus benefit from the principle of free movement of goods. In accordance with Article 168 paragraph 4 letter c TFEU, this regulation sets high standards for the quality and safety of medical devices, among other things by ensuring that data obtained from clinical trials are reliable and robust and that the safety of trial participants is protected." (Regulation (EU) 2017/745 of the European Parliament and of the Council of 5 April 2017 on medical devices, 2017)

Medical device law (Medical Device Regulation) regulates the clinical evaluation of medical devices. The MEDDEV 2.7.1 (Rev. 4) guide to clinical evaluation.

CE Marking of Products

Throughout the entire development process of products and procedures, an assessment and evaluation of the achieved interim results is carried out. This cyclical process extends over all phases from the idea to the finished product. This approach is clearly shown in Fig. 6.16.

The evaluations are carried out according to agreed criteria, which can be divided into the following groups:

- Fixed requirements, standards to be met
- Minimum requirements
- Customer requests see pp. 100–102 in Busch (2003a, pp. 100–102)

In general, the following criteria are particularly taken into account:

- Performance parameters
- Operability
- Availability of the materials and assemblies used
- Dimensions and weight
- Transportability
- Suitability for maintenance

The assessment should not only consider.

- the current development object, but also
- the entire system in which the object is integrated and

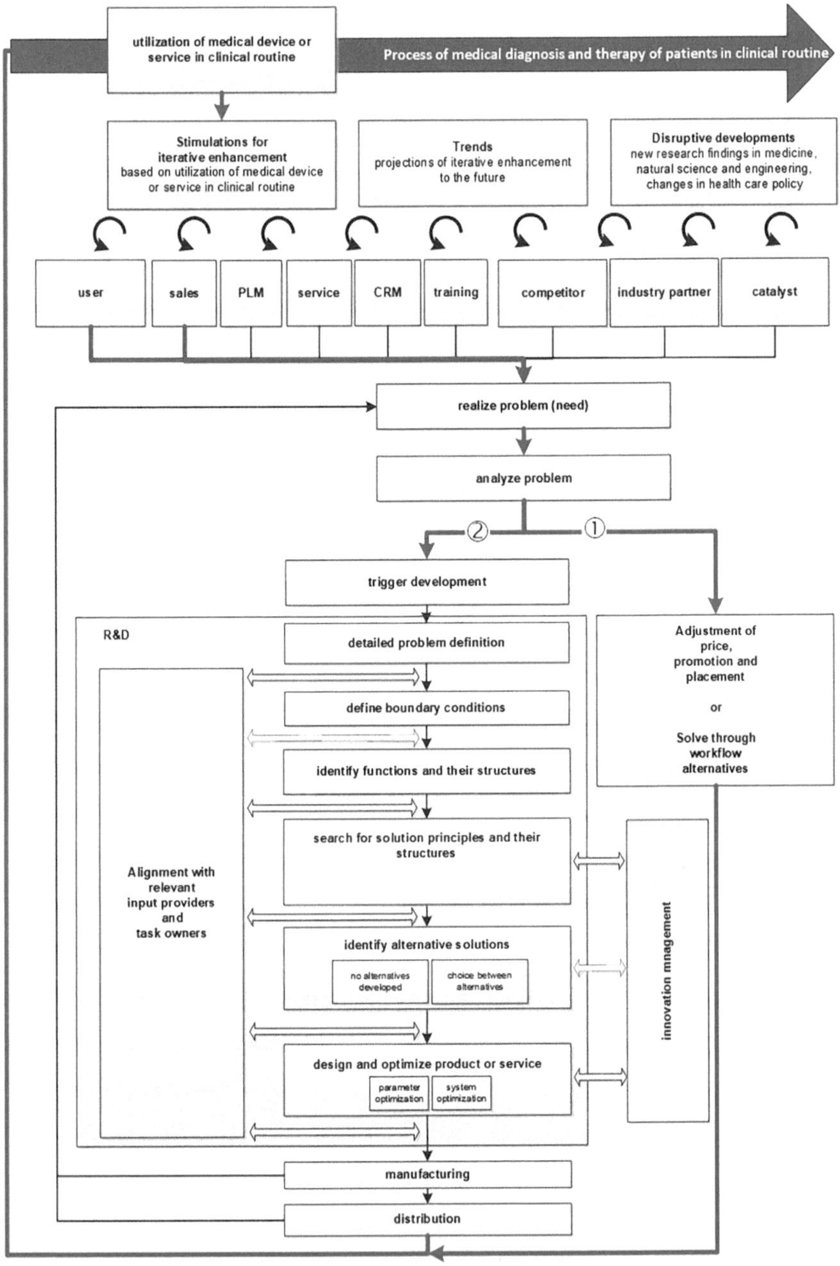

Fig. 6.16 Innovation and development process. (Adapted from Busch, 2021)

- also take into account the product life cycle from raw material extraction, energy supply to recycling or disposal, taking into account
- sustainability

include.

The EC marking and EN ISO 14971 also focus particularly on the following criteria:

- Safety in the use of the product
- Consumer protection, risk to patients and users
- Probability of risks and accidents occurring
- Proactive measures for risk control
- Environmental protection
- Sustainability

It makes sense to pay attention to the concerns of the CE marking in all interim evaluations in the development process.

The CE marking is intended to help ensure the free movement of goods within the European Economic Area (EEA). This marking is not a quality mark and does not indicate the origin of the product. It is therefore also considered an administrative mark. The CE mark only confirms that the requirements of all relevant EU directives have been met for the product in question.

The CE marking was already introduced in 1985 by a decision of the EC Council.

In 1993, the decision on the modules to be used in the technical harmonization directives for the various phases of the conformity assessment procedures and the rules for the affixing and use of the CE conformity marking was published. (*Decision on the modules to be used in the technical Harmonization guidelines for the modules to be used for the various phases of conformity assessment procedures and the rules for the affixing and use of the CE conformity marking*, 1993)

Regulation (EC) No. 765/2008 of the European Parliament and of the Council of 09.07.2008 formulates the following objective:

> "(1) It must be ensured that products benefiting from the free movement of goods within the Community meet requirements for a high level of protection of public interests such as general health and safety, occupational health and safety, consumer and environmental protection, and security, while at the same time ensuring that the free movement of goods is not restricted beyond the level permitted by the harmonization legislation of the Community or other relevant Community regulations. Therefore, provisions for accreditation, market surveillance, controls of products from third countries, and CE marking should be provided.
>
> (2) An overarching framework of regulations and principles for accreditation and market surveillance must be established. This framework should leave untouched the substantive provisions of existing legislation, which set out the requirements for the protection of public interests such as health, safety, consumer and environmental protection, and should rather aim to improve their application.
>
> (3) This Regulation should be considered as a supplement to Decision No. 768/2008/EC of the European Parliament and of the Council of 9 July 2008 on a common legal framework for the marketing of products." (REGULATION (EC) No. 765/2008 OF THE EUROPEAN PARLIAMENT AND OF THE COUNCIL on the rules for accreditation and market surveillance in connection with the marketing of products and repealing Regulation (EEC), 2008)

On 16.07.2021, Regulation 765/2008 was updated.

For **medical devices**—as for all product groups—special guidelines for CE marking apply. In Germany, the following guidelines are particularly important:

For **medical devices** (MDD) the Directive 93/42/EEC of 14 June 1993 on medical devices

> "Medical devices must provide a high level of protection for patients, users, and third parties and achieve the performance specified by the manufacturer. Maintaining or improving the level of protection achieved in the Member States is one of the essential objectives of this Directive." (DIRECTIVE 93/42/EEC OF THE COUNCIL of 14 June 1993 on medical devices, 1993, p. 2)

This directive was updated by

- Directive 98/79/EC of the European Parliament and of the Council of 27 October 1998 L 331 1 07.12.1998
- Directive 2000/70/EC of the European Parliament and of the Council of 16 November 2000 L 313 22 13.12.2000
- Directive 2001/104/EC of the European Parliament and of the Council of 7 December 2001 L 6 50 10.01.2002
- Regulation (EC) No. 1882/2003 of the European Parliament and of the Council of 29 September 2003 L 284 1 31.10.2003
- Directive 2007/47/EC of the European Parliament and of the Council of 5 September 2007 L 247 21 21.09.2007

For **active implantable medical devices** (AIMDD) the Directive 90/385/EEC of the Council of 20 June 1990 on the approximation of the laws of the Member States relating to active implantable medical devices published in the Official Journal No. L 189 of 20/07/1990 p. 0017–0036

> "Active implantable medical devices must provide a high level of safety to patients, users, and third parties and achieve the specified performance level when implanted into the human body.
>
> The following definitions apply to this Directive:
>
> a) Medical device: all instruments, apparatus, devices, substances or other objects used individually or in combination, including the accessories and software necessary for the proper functioning of the device, which are intended by the manufacturer for use in humans for the following purposes:
>
> - Detection, prevention, monitoring, treatment or alleviation of diseases or injuries,
> - Investigation, replacement or modification of the anatomy or a physiological process, or
> - Contraception,
>
> and whose intended primary function is not achieved by pharmacological, chemical or immunological means or by metabolism, but whose function can be supported by such means.
>
> b) Active medical device: any medical device whose operation depends on an electrical energy source or another energy source other than that directly generated by the human body or gravity.
>
> c) Active implantable medical device: any active medical device designed to be fully or partially introduced into the human body by a surgical or medical procedure or through a natural body opening and intended to remain there after the procedure." (Council Directive 90/385/EEC of 20 June 1990 on the approximation of the laws of the Member States on active implantable medical devices, 1990)

Procedure for preparation and implementation of EC marking

For the EC marking procedure, consultant-specific steps are recommended by the various consultants and Notified Bodies.

The following sequence of steps can be derived from the relevant directives.

- Classifying the product to be marked into the appropriate risk class
- Compilation of the relevant EU directives, standards and other legal regulations (An overview of these is available.
- Preparation of the technical documentation developed during the development process, including the user manual
- Documentation of the risk management system used during development, manufacturing, and preparation for distribution, according to EN ISO 14971
- Preparation and realization of a possibly required
- clinical evaluation
- Identification of a suitable Notified Body through research at the German Accreditation Body (DAkkS) and collaboration with a Notified Body, if specified in the relevant CE directive
- If required by EU directive, provide proof of compliance with legal requirements. Fulfillment of the basic and other legal requirements in a conformity assessment procedure (possibly together with the Notified Body).
- Affixing of the CE mark by the manufacturer before the product is placed on the market

The path to the CE mark is particularly demanding for first-time applications, but can be managed with a realistic time effort. For companies dealing with CE marking, the Technology and Innovation Consultation of the Chamber of Commerce offers assistance and support for all questions related to the practical application of EU legal regulations and standards.

Consequences for the manufacturer of the product

From the start of development work, the relevant EU directives must be identified and complied with. In addition, all legal regulations must be taken into account.

The personnel involved in the development, manufacturing, and distribution of the product must be thoroughly informed and trained.

In all cyclical development and evaluation phases, the criteria must be set so that the directives for EC marking are met.

If EC marking has already been carried out in the company, the existing experienced personnel should be involved in new procedures and the existing networks to the required partner institutions should be utilized.

If EC marking is to be carried out for the first time, it is recommended to consult suitable advisors (Chamber of Commerce, authorities, TÜV, lawyers) as the process of EC marking requires a significant effort.

6.5 Implementation and Distribution

6.5.1 From Manufacturing to Application

In the previous sections of this book, we were able to trace the path from recognizing the problem to the completion of the product. If the idea is to develop into an innovation, the step from the manufacturer to the user must be taken.

These paths depend on,

- whether the problem became apparent in practice, i.e., the stimulus for iterative development results from the use of an already existing product or procedure
- or whether the development project is based on disruptive development from current research findings and trends.

In Fig. 6.17 these two possibilities are illustrated.

If the impetus for problem-solving or a specific task for the development of a product, which is intended to supplement or optimize existing systems, is provided by the user, or is specified together with the service, sales or consultants of a manufacturer, we use the term **Implementation** in this context.

In this case, no separate marketing is required, as the user is already involved in the innovation process.

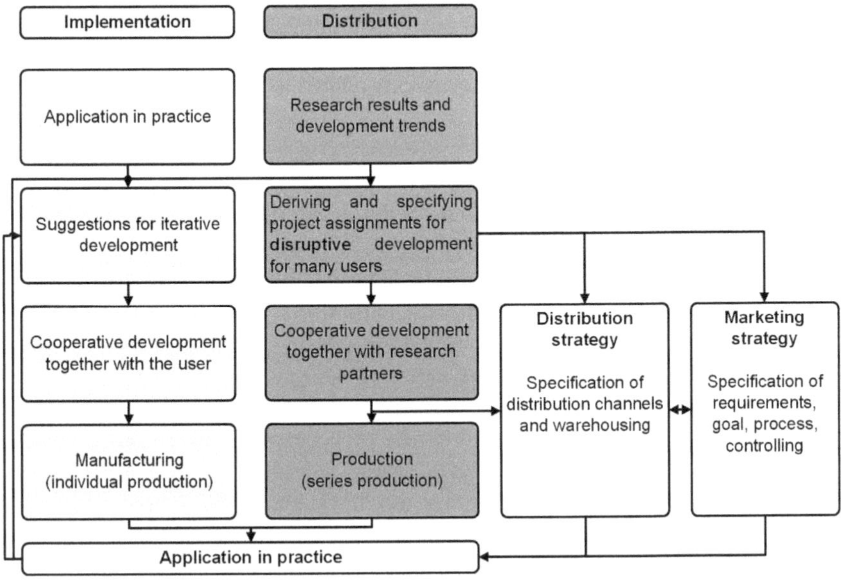

Fig. 6.17 Implementation and Distribution

If it becomes apparent during product development that the product would be suitable for a broad potential user pool, the product development can be aligned towards serial production.

If the idea for product development arises from research findings or can be identified from the current development trend, an order for a **disruptive** development can be given. The development and production are then aligned towards a broad potential user pool. This results in the need to strategically plan a **Distribution** and thus develop a marketing strategy and a sales strategy.

6.5.2 Developing the Distribution Strategy

Distribution characterizes the process of transferring products to the users of these products. It includes all activities that are realized between the activities of the manufacturer—i.e., recognizing the problem situation, product development, manufacturing, and maintenance—up to the use by the user.

In distribution, marketing and sales are closely intertwined.

The **marketing** is based on a detailed and forward-looking **market analysis**. The insights from this analysis flow into both the formulation of the development order and the cooperative development—together with the cooperation and research partners.

The market analysis is—in connection with the company strategy—also the basis for the formulation of the **marketing goals** and the selection of the **marketing instruments**. The entire process must be integrated into the company's management control system.

Marketing continuously receives information and impulses from the use of the products by the user. The **Maintenance** can support marketing through its user-friendly customer communication.

The **Sales** particularly includes

- defining the sales channels,
- warehousing,
- transport and
- delivery service.

6.6 Acquiring and Teaching of Innovation Competence

6.6.1 Lifelong Acquisition of Innovation Competence

The previous sections presented a versatile and extensive knowledge that should and can offer guidance and support in the development and realization of inventions and innovations.

Let us remember how Mephistopheles robs the eager student of some illusions:

"Grey, dear friend, is all theory, and green is the golden tree of life." (by Goethe, 1953)

We also know: Owning a cookbook does not automatically make you a gourmet chef, and knowing traffic signs does not replace a driving license.

So, more is required for successful action.

In Chap. 1 five creativity rules are mentioned and in Sect. 6.1 these rules were supplemented by ten innovation rules.

Overview

With an invention, a significant result has been achieved. This achievement—as significant as it may be—is initially merely the starter's permission for another challenging hurdle race, which should ideally only end with the successful introduction to the market.

As support and encouragement for this new challenge, we will present ten rules of innovation in this chapter.

A necessary prerequisite for achieving innovation is professional project management, coupled with effective management control. However, it should first be estimated what prospects the innovation might have on the market and which strategy for its realization is sensible and promising. A market growth-market share-matrix can serve as a decision-making tool. This matrix can simultaneously serve as a basis for developing a protective rights strategy to secure intellectual property. The work on protective rights is significantly facilitated if an appropriate infrastructure is available, in which both patent engineers and patent attorneys are involved.

In many cases, it is advisable to first test the mode of operation of the proposed innovation with a sample or functional model. This allows important conclusions to be drawn for the continuation of this project, and misdevelopments can be more easily excluded in a forward-looking manner.

A particular hurdle on the way to market introduction is the approval of the products. This applies to both the clinical approval of medical devices and the general CE marking. The preparation for the approvals is not a one-time action, but extends through all phases of product development.

The most important criterion for whether an idea becomes an innovation is decided at the step from the manufacturer to the user. The necessary implementation and distribution include both marketing and sales and service.

Accompanying all steps from recognizing a problem to introducing a product to the market is the acquisition of the necessary innovation competence among all involved actors. Lifelong learning and project-integrated competence acquisition play an important role in this. Learning, in turn, requires the availability of suitable teaching and learning materials as well as the creation of learning-demanding and learning-promoting conditions. In this chapter, practical experiences from the authors' many years of research and design work are conveyed.

We need more than theoretical knowledge.

Important!
Successfully navigating the path from the identified problem to the market-ready product requires not only knowledge but also skills, abilities, and personal commitment—it requires innovation competence.

The foundation for innovation competence is laid in childhood.

The early childhood years are fundamental for acquiring knowledge and values as well as for learning how to learn.

Listening to stories or reading fairy tales trains the ability to listen attentively and conveys not only knowledge but also norms and values. The following statements are quoted regarding the importance of fairy tales in the development of children:

Albert Einstein: "*If you want intelligent children, read them fairy tales. If you want even more intelligent children, read them even more fairy tales.*" (Einstein, 2013)

Johann Gottfried von Herder: "*A child who has never been told fairy tales will have a piece of field in his soul where nothing can be grown in later years.*" (Johann Gottfried Herder, 2021)

Not only in childhood—but also in professional training and further education—personal experiences, anecdotes or other events can not only lighten up the learning material, but also support the memory of the material (and of the teachers).

Learning has predominantly been through observation, comprehension (in the true sense of the word), and imitation for many millennia.

This becomes clear when we consider learning in the Hanseatic era (see first example, Chap. 5).

The economic and cultural conditions (i.e., the learning-demanding situations) also had to adapt to the learning culture in the Hanseatic cities. Particularly formative for professional development were the activities in the foreign offices of the Hanseatic League. The contacts with merchants from partner cities and the kinesthetic-oriented "grasping and tackling" in their own workshops and trading houses prepared the children and adolescents for their later tasks.

If the Hanseatic League was able to remain stable for several centuries and successfully adapt to all conditions and situations, this testifies to the fact that the Hanseatic people possessed solid creative competencies.

Learning through all senses from an early age was revived by Friedrich Fröbel with his educational concept (Sauerbrey & Winkler, 2018).

With their playthings, children should independently acquire knowledge about their environment. Adults are encouraged to participate in the play and communicate in the process. The children's imagination and fantasy are promoted, and their motor skills are developed.

The playthings include balls; in addition, there are cylinders and cubes as well as other building blocks. The toys are built on familiar elements, and gradually the toys are expanded by newly added elements. The playthings are still available for purchase today.

In times of war and crisis, due to the existing shortage, the toys were made by parents, siblings, or grandparents themselves, or the children invented their own toys from pieces of wood, sticks, old screws, or pieces of paper and fabric, and played with them enthusiastically and creatively.

Under the conditions of a (partial) abundance and oversupply in an "affluent society", there is currently a "race" among the givers for the largest and most expensive playthings. The preference is to hand over completely finished ("Don't break it!") and possibly electronically controlled toys.

The entire family is proud when even the youngest can "swipe" across the screen and present the image series to the amazed viewers. The imagination and the development of "craft" skills are only given a chance when the gifts are (secretly) disassembled.

The current and still expected scientific-technical development and the associated changes in the world of work, however, require that the possibilities of these techniques be used early on and the necessary competencies be acquired.

Touch was also mentioned as a channel for information intake. This was probably misunderstood by many generations of teachers (and parents) and primarily related to the effect of the cane.

Those who will not hear must feel.

How widespread touch was used as a learning-promoting tool is described by Mailly in the German Legal Antiquities: "*The boundaries of a property, a community have been strictly supervised since ancient times.*" (Maily, 1929, p. 61)

> "The boundary stones are chalked by each community on their side and the present boys receive a slap or their ears are pulled as in old times, so that they remember the boundaries (Raine) as descendants , as they are still told today ... This is also called the boundary stone mark." (Maily, 1929, p. 64)

From the experiences of many generations of learners and teachers, procedures have been collected and tested that can contribute to making learning successful and effective.

- Parents crafting together with their children and crafting in child care should be a matter of course.
- In school, it is important that the acquisition of basic competencies is at least equal to the transmission of (too) extensive factual knowledge. Methodological

knowledge and general education must not be neglected. The project method offers many possibilities for this.

- Outside of school, visiting scientific and technical collections and museums can stimulate creative thinking and action (which also includes crafting).
- Reading adventure books (e.g., Robinson Crusoe by Daniel Defoe), fantasy stories, and historical novels also train the imagination and stimulate thinking in problem-solving.
- In studies, the acquisition of methodological knowledge and thinking in system and process contexts—as already in general education schools—must be given more space. Internships and dual studies offer favorable conditions for this.
- In professional further education and in lifelong learning as a whole, project-integrated (or project-related) competence acquisition should play a dominant role.

In the research and design work of the ITF Schwerin (Busch, 2017), the following insights were gained from the analysis of vocational training and further education projects, among other things:

- "The acquisition of methodological and social competence and the ability for self-directed learning is not (still) given the necessary importance in vocational training and further education.
- The learning culture and especially the learning infrastructure in companies are not or not sufficiently oriented towards self-directed, project-integrated learning.
- External innovation and learning process support is only realized in exceptional cases.
- The learning and teaching materials used do not yet sufficiently take into account the possibilities of modern information and communication technology (e.g., apps, e-books, interactive whiteboards, multi-touch tables, multi-media learning and exhibition spaces) and the constantly changing usage habits for these technologies across all population segments.
- The transfer of modern findings from educational and innovation research often only takes place in time-limited model projects.
- Regional learning cultures are not, or not sufficiently, considered in their complexity and especially in their interaction with corporate learning cultures." (Busch, 2017, pp. 162–163)

Increasingly, traditional organizational structures and work methods

- with a defined starting situation for innovation processes,
- a goal with firmly agreed target parameters and
- a predetermined processing process

cannot always meet the growing demands on innovation processes.

Project processing in "well-trodden paths" is not sufficiently effective. The term "team" in the sense of a horse or ox team may certainly fit departments with little innovative ambition, but it should not be used for creatively working groups, as they should not be driven by a coachman in worn-out wagon tracks.

Rather, flexible working methods are required that more closely resemble the hunting behavior of packs, and in which the individual group members, according to their special abilities,

- highly motivated,
- independently,
- but acting in a coordinated manner and
- in constant communication with each other

effectively participate in achieving the goal.

There is a contradiction between the goals and contents of the innovation processes and the traditional methods and organizational forms for developing innovations.

New goals and contents require the application of adequate methods, organizational forms, and competencies.

The following section therefore provides some pointers on how to design the imparting of innovation competence.

6.6.2 Integrated Project Delivery of Innovation Competence

In higher education and technical colleges, students acquire professional competencies that enable them for a successful career start. The ability to realize innovations is usually not sufficiently developed.

Therefore, as early as 1959, LOHMANN called for a course, … "which could be described as 'Productive Thinking' or 'Creative Work'." (Lohmann, 1960).

A thorough analysis of engineering education with a view to its redesign was presented by Buggenhagen in 1987 (Buggenhagen, 1987).

The quality of the methodological training of engineers and scientists has not significantly improved in the meantime. Therefore, continuing professional development in the process of concrete project work in companies continues to be of great importance.

This results in market opportunities for educational companies, but also new requirements. The key to a qualitative further development of educational companies is first and foremost the development of a company vision and a company strategy. The personnel and organizational development of educational companies for this promising task is a long-term process, which is associated with an expansion or renewal of the staff.

The trainers, supervisors, and consultants of educational companies must learn **how to teach** and **how to learn**.

Educational companies that want to offer the development of innovation capability, especially in small and medium-sized enterprises, as a service, must, according to our experience, have the following characteristics:

- They must be able to recognize the actual innovation needs of the companies and, together with the company, derive the required competence needs from them.
- They must be able to offer process-accompanying and simultaneous professional competence development of employees and learning in the company for technical and organizational innovations in companies.
- They must have established cooperative relationships with business consultants and other institutions with which they can jointly realize comprehensive business support.
- They must place the employee at the center of didactic-methodological concepts and practice modern methods of competence acquisition. Learning primarily takes place integrated into projects and based on real work and problem situations of the customer.
- They must convey the theoretical content with modern self-learning media, with the help of which learners can access knowledge bases from any learning location.
- They must have a close relationship of trust with the companies they support.

The educational and consulting services are to be provided for the entire innovation process. They particularly cover the following areas:

- Introduction to innovation methodology
- Development of competence balances
- Identification of innovative problem situations
- Development of market analyses and marketing strategies
- Development of financing and funding strategies
- Development of intellectual property analyses
- Specification of innovative problem situations
- Development of innovative product and process ideas
- Evaluation of innovative solutions and strategies
- Development of innovation strategies
- Development of patents, utility models, and trademarks
- Development and realization of ways to improve individual development of creativity, mobility, and flexibility

The problem-solving process is inseparable from learning processes.

The interplay between the innovation process and the learning process is reflected in the combination of project work and learning, as shown in Fig. 6.18.

Project-integrated self-directed learning with modern information and communication tools is becoming increasingly important.

For the development of innovative solutions and their implementation in the market, the collaboration of several actors in innovation groups is indispensable in almost all cases.

An innovation group—as a creative collective—is a number of individuals with complementary competencies, who in direct contact—or connected via suitable media—work on such innovations that reflect a quantum leap in a development process (Busch, 2017).

Phases	Project management	Acquisition of skills
1. Recognizing the problem	– Perceiving the external demand – Searching for the core of the problem – Adopting the problem as a goal	– Acquire knowledge of analysis and forecasting techniques – Acquiring skills for obtaining information – Consolidation of behaviors (problem sensitivity)
2. Specifying the task	– Determining the goal, the environment, and the available potential – Considering and developing implementation options – Forming the project team	– Acquisition of methodological skills – Acquiring and consolidating project management and management support skills – Consolidation of behavioral patterns – Further development of teamwork skills
3. Developing solution variants	– Designing partial target sequences – Developing variants – Assessing consequences and side effects	– Acquisition of methodological skills (variant search, creativity techniques, modeling) – Expanding professional competence – Acquiring and consolidating the ability to work with simulation models – Further development of social skills
4. Evaluating the solution variants and making decisions	– Derive evaluation criteria – Evaluate – Deciding – Specifying the goal and the solution	– Acquiring skills in the application of assessment procedures and – Acquiring further social skills
5. Realization of the project	– Implementing the solution concept – Checking the processing progress – Documenting the result	– Acquire and consolidate the ability to use information and communication technologies in design and production processes – Acquire skills in the application of controlling – Consolidate the ability to manage projects and actively participate in the project group
6. Analysis of the project result	– Developing the target-result comparison – Analyzing and criticizing the approach and solution – Drawing on experience – Saving internal models – Deriving new problems	– Consolidating analytical skills – Developing critical faculties – Acquiring skills for presenting results (presentation techniques) – Consolidating communication skills

Fig. 6.18 Learning and working in the phases of the innovation process

A multidisciplinary composition with different but complementary competencies of the employees is beneficial for achieving original solution ideas and for a comprehensive consideration of the interrelationships of the process circumstances and the process result including the impact assessment (Busch, 1993; Heyse, 1984).

In Chap. 5, example 5 describes a successful work of innovation groups. This example shows how learning and working on real research problems can be conducted and how scientific and social creativity can be developed together.

Learning takes place—integrated into the innovation process—as self-directed learning and is supported by external experts. The problem-solving process is carried out in the unity of group work and individual work.

This example shows that external innovation and learning support not only relieves companies, but also enables them to improve their competitiveness.

Acquiring the necessary competencies for an effective design of innovation processes is continuously—starting in general education schools through training to professional continuing education—to be integrated into the learning processes.

This requires appropriate empowerment of teachers and the supervisors and company leaders.

When comparing the dramaturgy of teaching and the methodology of inventing, the following **analogies** become clear:

- Both processes start with a problem situation.
- To solve the problem (conflict, contradiction), a tension field is built up.
- The goal must be clearly defined.
- To solve the problem, inertia resistance must be overcome. Interest and enthusiasm need to be aroused.
- The basis for problem-solving is the collective action of the participants.
- The problem-solving process requires guidance.
- Creative methods are used to solve the problem.
- The tension is resolved through a surprising effect.
- The result of the process leads to not only an increase in subject-specific knowledge but also the further development of methodological competence and social skills.
- The solution to the problem reveals new problems and subsequent tasks to be addressed.

In addition to these analogies, both processes have **interactions**, which can be consciously utilized.

- The process of inventing is inseparable from learning processes. The conscious application of the dramaturgy of teaching can significantly support the process of leading (interdisciplinary and heterogeneous) groups in developing innovations (Operational Suggestion System, Quality Circles, Research Groups).
- Furthermore, understanding inventions in the context of education and training can help arouse interest in the subject matter, better understand its further development, and simultaneously acquire knowledge about the application of creative methods (Innovation Methodology).

Learning forms in innovation processes include both learning in courses and seminars (especially regarding methodological basics) as well as informal and implicit learning.

Informal learning plays a special role in innovation processes. It is not pure experiential learning, as theoretical basics that were not previously individually available also need to be acquired.

Research results from the ITF Schwerin suggest that learning in courses (and at conferences) only accounts for about 5% of learning in innovation processes. The remaining 95% is roughly evenly divided between informal and implicit learning. However, the proportions in funding policy and traditional continuing education research show a reverse relationship; resources and potentials are almost exclusively focused on learning in continuing education courses.

By merging project work and learning as well as work organization and learning organization, favorable conditions for a permanent current motivation to develop innovations are created.

The acquisition of competence for innovation processes can be significantly optimized through project-integrated learning. This requires new behaviors, attitudes, and competences from educational companies, company leaders, and educational staff.

The analysis of the innovation process reveals that corporate culture, problem-solving behavior (including innovation culture), and learning culture are closely interrelated and mutually dependent.

Corporate culture particularly includes value perceptions, behavioral norms, knowledge stocks, problem-solving behavior, and learning culture (Busch, 2003b).

Developing the ability to innovate is becoming increasingly important for small and medium-sized enterprises in Germany as a key factor in securing competitiveness and the existence of companies. This can also prevent the one-sided "migration" of industrial potentials to low-wage countries and resource-rich regions.

Developing the ability to innovate is not just a new field of activity for educational companies. It is an option for maintaining the competitiveness of small and medium-sized enterprises and thus also

- political decision-makers,
- actors in the entire education system,
- the individual,
- companies and all regional actors who shape the regional learning culture,

are equally challenged.

Tip

For leaders in companies, the task is to develop a culture that promotes innovation, enabling the creative potential of all employees to be awakened and mobilized.

The education system, in turn, must ensure that the creative potential of children is recognized and promoted from preschool age. In general education schools and initial vocational training, it is particularly important to develop methodological competence and social skills. Children and young people should be involved in age-appropriate and challenging creative projects at an early stage.

The integration of vocational training and company further education can also make a significant contribution to the development of innovation capability in small and medium-sized enterprises.

6.7 Implementing the Innovation Methodology

6.7.1 Fields of Innovation

In the preceding sections of this book, we have particularly dealt with innovation processes in technology, specifically medical technology.

However, innovations are possible—and often necessary—in all areas of life.

To illustrate, consider

- the hairstylist who creates a new hairstyle,
- the florist who presents a special floral arrangement,
- the artists of all fields,
- the composers with their compositions,
- the architects of all styles,
- the gardener who breeds a new apple variety, or
- the playing child who builds a castle for his knights out of used cardboard boxes.

The following inventions in medicine are well known:

- the development and use of penicillin as an antibiotic from the discovery of the effect of mold on bacteria,
- the development of aspirin from the inherited knowledge of the Celts and Germans about the effect of vine bark,
- the vaccination against smallpox,
- the development of anesthesia procedures,
- organ transplantation, and
- embryo transfer.

In medicine, the interaction between the development of medical (biological) procedures and the development of medical technology is particularly evident. Illustrative examples include:

- the development of X-ray machines and their use in diagnosis and therapy,
- the use of embryo transfer and the development of the transfer device system,
- the construction of surgical robots and their use, for example, in microsurgery, and
- the construction of orthopedic aids and the further development of treatment procedures.

Innovative approaches in military strategy and tactics have often led to unexpected and decisive results. Examples that come to mind include

- Hannibal's crossing of the Alps with 37 war elephants (218 BC),
- Alexander's battle order and tactics in the Battle of Gaugamela (331 BC), and
- the use of "Greek fire" as an incendiary weapon in the Crusades.

... and even Casanova would not have been so successful had he not mastered and used the creative means of variation and combination.

For the individual areas of application—the fields of innovation—there may be specific modifications of the innovation methodology that result from legal regulations, profession-specific habits, or special boundary conditions.

6.7.2 Distribution Paths for Successful Use of the Methodology

The distribution paths result from the respective distribution strategy. Since in the present case the availability of the methodology in versatile areas of application is aimed for, there are

- several adjacent, complementary distribution channels
- with goal-oriented rational adjustments

possible and necessary.

The direct, individual-oriented, method of providing the available material can be particularly

- from personal recommendations,
- from targeted research,
- from advertising in professional literature and other media as well as
- from book presentations and readings

result.

Much more diverse are the paths across several bridges to the potential innovator and inventor.

For students in **general education schools** subject-specific modules of innovation methodology can be used, which should preferably also be integrated into project work. An interesting and vividly presented example is described in the book "Bees in Education forsustainable development" (Busch et al., 2021a, b).

The use of the variation method and the combination method is usually a lot of fun for students and is almost playfully executed.

This path requires that the teachers and supervisors during their training and also in their professional development got to know the innovation method and were able to practice it themselves. The necessary material must be available for them.

The innovation methodology can be incorporated much more intensively and goal-oriented into the **natural science subjects** in the higher grades of general education schools. The material can be used in the application of the project method and in project work as learning material and as practical guidance. This requires both

- availability of the material and
- the training of teachers in this field during their studies

prerequisite.

For school and extracurricular **working groups and project groups** (e.g. "Youth researches") the innovation methodology can provide important guidance. Accompanying consultation and the provision of the material are appropriate.

At **university**—and especially in dual studies—innovation methodology belongs in all technical, scientific, and business directions as its own (and connected with the other subjects) subject in the study plan. The interdisciplinary intertwining arises, for example, when it is shown from a business perspective that innovations are necessary, and at the same time it is shown how suitable innovations can be achieved in interdisciplinary work. Getting to know such procedures is advantageous in later use in companies (also personally).

In internships and in student work (especially in Bachelor's and Master's theses) emphasis should be placed on the application of suitable modules of innovation methodology.

Similar to general education schools, here too both

- the availability of the material and
- the training of teachers in this field during the studies

are required.

In professional **training and further education,** the teachers and mentors must have such competencies that they can enable the learners to actively participate in the innovation work and possibly also contribute to the development of inventions. Exemplary are courses, as described in Chap. 5 (Example 4).

The company's executives must themselves be convinced of the effectiveness of innovation methodology and support the educational work as best as possible (in their own interest).

The material for innovation methodology must be available for the employees in the companies and possibly be aligned with the specifics of the companies.

The versatile distribution paths are to be considered in the distribution strategy for the dissemination and effective use of the innovation strategy.

Cooperation with all levels of education policy and education institutions is indispensable to fully exploit the potential of the innovation methodology.

The mere publication of a book cannot effectively promote its cause.

6.7.3 Promoting the Use of Innovation Methodology

In the Middle Ages, wizards and alchemists were tasked with procuring desired or urgently needed items. They sometimes achieved remarkable results, even if these did not usually correspond to the original task. Among other things, European porcelain and gunpowder were reinvented.

Currently, inventors are expected to “conjure up” new ideas and products.

Over the past approximately 150 years, an interesting correlation has been observed between the respective political and economic situation on the one hand and the development and application of innovation methodology, as well as the number of patents filed on the other hand can be seen.

It is in the interest of individual companies and the state to dynamically advance technical, economic, and business development through innovations. Therefore, it is essential to promote and stimulate the motivation and competencies of employees to improve the competitiveness of companies.

Since about the middle of the nineteenth century, there have been approaches in Germany to reward suggestions for improvements made by workers. In addition to financial compensation, ideal recognition plays an important role.

Alfred Krupp was one of the first companies to introduce a binding regulation.

In the mid-1930s, the company suggestion system was strongly promoted in Germany to save labor, material, and energy.

Since 1957, the law on employee inventions has regulated the recognition and protection of inventions and technical improvement suggestions made by employees in the private and public sectors, as well as by civil servants and soldiers: “*Law on Employee Inventions in the version published in the Federal Law Gazette Part III, classification number 422-1, last amended by Article 25 of the law of July 7, 2021 (BGBl. I S. 2363)*”.

A distinction is made between inventions (which are patentable or eligible for utility model protection) and technical improvement suggestions.

In addition to the immediate economic goals, the suggestions can and should also take into account occupational safety, environmental protection, work organization, marketing, and corporate culture.

As a logical step in the further development of the company suggestion system to an idea management system, it was classified into corporate management and the shaping of corporate culture.

Idea management is characterized by

- the transition from the individual proposer to the creative collective,
- the need to shape a creatively oriented corporate culture, with a particular focus on including customers and suppliers,
- the inclusion of relevant structural units of the company (design, marketing, service, procurement, etc.)

Idea management aims to involve all employees and fully exploit their competencies. It is part of the broader innovation management, which is particularly focused on more fundamental and comprehensive innovations.

In the chain of people involved from identifying the problem to solving it, the following actors should also be considered:

Impulse generators
The role of impulse **generators** was discussed in Sect. 1.7. They are important for the market-oriented control of innovation and development activities in companies.

Problem solvers
Based on the information about product problems, solutions are developed by the problem solvers in the iterative innovation and development process.

Liaison person
Once the information is available to the responsible process actors in the company, it is important that it is prioritized and passed on to the group(s) that can take up these suggestions and use them for further development. In this role, the liaison person assumes,

- that universities and student work can be taken into account,
- that targeted competence development of employees is necessary,
- that creativity techniques are consciously used, and
- that suitable idea storage and idea management are developed and implemented.

It should be made possible for this group of people in particular to acquire basic competencies in the relevant modules of innovation management. Motivation should be promoted and all possibilities for material and ideal support should be exhausted.

Ancient experience teaches us: **Situations that promote innovation are more activating and effective than merely favorable conditions.**

To put it briefly: **Challenge is the most effective form of promotion. Necessity is the mother of invention.**

Key Insights of the Chapter

- The decision to transform an invention into an innovation initiates a comprehensive and multifaceted process with high demands on **Innovation Management**.
- Leadership must rely heavily on the available **Instruments of Management Control**.
- The **Intellectual Property Activities** carried out during the development of the invention must be continuously pursued, as new ideas for the product and processes emerge in all phases of the project work, for which intellectual property must be secured. The granting and use of licenses expand the responsible work area of patent engineers and patent attorneys.
- The availability of testing opportunities proves to be useful and necessary for testing ideas before their introduction into the implementation phase. For technical products and processes, dedicated or contractually bound

laboratories and **Model Workshops** have proven to be effective.
- Throughout all phases of the innovation process, the **CE Marking** must be considered and ensured by management. In the fields of medicine and medical technology, special requirements apply to the obligation to label.
- Since an invention only becomes an innovation on the market, the **Distribution** with all its sub-areas, using the existing operational experiences and available distribution channels, must be activated in a timely manner.
- Without the necessary competencies among all those involved in the innovation project, success cannot be achieved. The foundation for the development of **Innovation Competence** is laid in general education schools.
- Professional training must be supplemented by ongoing competence acquisition integrated into the work in an era of dynamic scientific and economic development. The **Education System** must itself continue to innovate.

References

Bär, C., Fiege, J., & Weiß, M. (2017). *Anwendungsbezogenes Projektmanagement* (1st ed.). Springer Vieweg. https://doi.org/10.1007/978-3-662-52974-4.

Böhm, J. (2019). *Erfolgsfaktor Agilität: Warum Scrum und Kanban zu zufriedenen Mitarbeitern und erfolgreichen Kunden führen*. Springer Vieweg. https://doi.org/10.1007/978-3-658-25085-0.

Brandstäter, J. (2013). *Agile IT-Projekte erfolgreich gestalten*. Springer Vieweg. https://doi.org/10.1007/978-3-658-04430-5.

Buggenhagen, H. J. (1987). *Ingenieurausbildung—neue Ansprüche und Lösungsansätze aus hoch schuldidaktischer Sicht*.

Busch, E. (2009). *Lecture "Entwicklung innovativer Medizintechnik" at the 3rd Conference on Precision Engineering Design*.

Busch, E. (2021). *Dissertation "Optimierung des Innovations- und Entwicklungsprozesses von bio medizintechnischen Geräten"*.

Busch, E., Busch, K. H., Lehmann, F., Greulich, A., Busch, H., & Becker, K. (2021). *Bienen in der Bildung für nachhaltige Entwicklung*. epubli.

Busch, E., Strobel, N., Nobach, K., Bulitta, C., Hirshfeld, J., Wu, L., & de Abreu, M. (2021). Optimizing the innovation and development process of medical devices—A study based on angiographic equipment. *Health and Technology, 11*(3), 563–574. https://doi.org/10.1007/s12553-021-00537-7.

Busch, K. H. (1993). *Kreativitätstraining in der DDR*. 116–127–116–127.

Busch, K. H. (2003a). *Innovationen erfolgreich realisieren: Erfinden lernen—lernend erfinden*. trafo.

Busch, K. H. (2003b). *Lernen in Innovationsprozessen* (Vol. 4).

Busch, K. H. (2017). *Wandel der Arbeitswelt—Wandel der Innovationsprozesse*. itf.

Busch, K. H., & Busch, E. (2015). *Impulse der Feinwerktechnik auf den wissen-schaftlichen Gerä tebau der Agrarforschung*. TU Dresden.

Conrad, W. (1980). *Wer-Was-Wann: Entdeckungen und Erfindungen in Naturwissenschaft und Technik*. Fachbuchverlag.

Dechange, A. (2020). *Projektmanagement—Schnell erfasst* (1st ed.). Springer Gabler. https://doi.org/10.1007/978-3-662-57667-0.

Dufft, N., Remmel, U., & Breden, T. (2018). Neues Denken für Controller. *Controlling & Management Review, 62*(4), 34–39. https://doi.org/10.1007/s12176-018-0025-y.

Einstein, A. (2013). *Quote Fairy Tales*. www.spruchpool.de/. https://www.spruchpool.de/wenn-du-intelligente-kinder-willst-lies-ihnen-maerchen-vor/.

Entscheidung über die in den technischen Harmonisierungs¬richtlinien zu verwendenden Module für die verschiedenen Phasen der Konformitätsbewertungsverfahren und die Regeln für die An bringung und Verwendung der CE-Konformitätskennzeichnung. (1993).

Fiedler, R. (2020). *Controlling von Projekten: Mit konkreten Beispielen aus der Unternehmenspra xis—Alle controllingrelevanten Aspekte der Projektplanung, Projektsteuerung und Projektkon Trolle*. https://doi.org/10.1007/978-3-658-28032-1.

Fischer, T., Möller, K., & Schultze, W. (2015). *Controlling: Grundlagen, Instrumente und Entwicklungsperspektiven*. Schäffer-Poeschel.

Friedl, G., Hofmann, C., & Pedell, B. (2022). *Kostenrechnung: Eine entscheidungsorientierte Ein führung*. Vahlen. https://doi.org/10.15358/9783800668151.

Gleich, R., & Munck, J. C. (2021). Sechs Thesen zur Weiterentwicklung des Innovations-Control lings. *Controlling & Management Review, 65*(7), 8–15. https://doi.org/10.1007/s12176-021-0417-2.

von Goethe, J. W. (1953). *Faust*. Ohilipp Reclam.

Granig, P. (2007). Innovationsbewertung Potentialprognose und -steuerung durch Ertrags- und Ri sikosimulation. *Gabler*. https://doi.org/10.1007/978-3-8350-5412-7.

Heyse, V. (1984). *Grundlagen des wissenschaftlich-technischen Schöpfertums in Forschungs- und Entwicklungsprozessen*.

Horváth, P., Gleich, R., & Seiter, M. (2020). *Controlling* (14th ed.). Vahlen. https://www.vahlen.de/horvath-gleich-seiter-controlling/product/25337903.

Johann Gottfried Herder. (2021). *Johann Gottfried von Herder über Märchen*. gutezitate.com. https://gutezitate.com/zitat/223477.

Kaschny, M., Nolden, M., & Schreuder, S. (2015). *Innovationsmanagement im Mittelstand—Stra tegien, Praxisbeispiele* (1st ed.). Springer Gabler. https://doi.org/10.1007/978-3-658-02545-8.

König, W. (1997). *Propyläen Technikgeschichte* (Vol. 4, p. 328). Ulstein Buchverlage GmbH.

Kraus, G., & Westermann, R. (2019). *Projektmanagement mit System: Organisation, Methoden, Steuerung* (6th ed.). Springer Gabler. https://doi.org/10.1007/978-3-658-24521-4.

Kusay-Merkle, U. (2021). *Agiles Projektmanagement im Berufsalltag: Für mittlere und kleine Pro jekte* (2nd ed.). Springer Gabler.https://link.springer.com/book/10.1007/978-3-662-62810-2#bibliographic-information.

Kuster, J., Bachmann, C., Hubmann, M., Lippmann, R., & Schneider, P. (2022). *Handbuch Projekt management: Agil—Klassisch—Hybrid* (5th ed.). Springer Gabler. https://doi.org/10.1007/978-3-662-65473-6.

Landwehr-Zloch, S. (2022). *Management und Controlling von Innovationen: Wertorientierung im Kontext von Bewertungsunsicherheit und Komplexität* (pp. 1–21). https://doi.org/10.1007/978-3-658-04795-5_75-2.

Lohmann, H. (1960). *Zur Theorie und Praxis der Heuristik in der Ingenieurerziehung*.

Madauss, B. (2020). *Projektmanagement: Theorie und Praxis aus einer Hand* (8th ed.). Springer Vieweg. https://doi.org/10.1007/978-3-662-59384-4.

Maily, A. (1929). *Grenzsteinmark* (pp. 61 and 64). Reinhold.

Menze, S. (2013). Projekt-Controlling mit Earned Value und Earned Schedule. *Controlling & Management Review, 57*(3), 68–76. https://doi.org/10.1365/s12176-013-0759-5.

Möller, K., Schultze, W., & Steinmann, J.-C. (2016). Innovationscontrolling. In C. P. Hoffmann, S. Lennerts, C. Schmitz, W. Stölzle, & F. Uebernickel (Eds.), *Business Innovation: Das St. Galler Modell* (pp. 141–162). Springer Fachmedien. https://doi.org/10.1007/978-3-658-07167-7_10.

Möller, T. (2020). *Projektleiter/in—Pragmatischer Leitfaden für klassisches, agiles und hybrides Projektmanagement für Projektmanager/innen und alle Teammitglieder* (2nd ed.). con-thor. http://www.pm-experten.de/downloads/e-book_Projektleiter-in_Leitfaden%20 Projektmanagement_2Aufl_2020.pdf.

Nobach, K. (2010). Kennzahlengestütztes Risikocontrolling im Mittelstand. In G. Baier, G. Günther, G. Janke, & H. Muschol (Eds.), *Bewältigung von Unternehmensrisiken- Yearbook 2009/2010 of the Institute for Business Administration of the West Saxon University of Applied Sciences Zwickau* (pp. 115–134). Peter Lang. https://www.peterlang.com/document/1135508.

Nobach, K. (2019). Bedeutung der Digitalisierung für das Controlling und den Controller. In P. Ulrich & B. Baltzer (Eds.), *Value Creation in Business Administration: Festschrift for Prof. Dr. Habil. Wolfgang Becker on his 65th Birthday* (pp. 247–269). Springer Fachmedien. https://doi.org/10.1007/978-3-658-18573-2_11.

Nobach, K. (2021). Projektcontrolling in der Unternehmenspraxis. In W. Becker & P. Ulrich (Eds.), *Praxishandbuch Controlling* (pp. 1–28). Springer Fachmedien. https://doi.org/10.1007/978-3-658-04795-5_72-1.

Nobach, K., & Immel, C. (2017). Vom Controller zum Business-Partner bei Bosch. *Controlling & Management Review, 61*(3), 78–85. https://doi.org/10.1007/s12176-017-0044-0.

Noé, M. (2017). *Mit Controlling zum Projekterfolg* (2nd ed.). Springer Gabler. https://doi.org/10.1007/978-3-658-14799-0.

Prowareness. (Ed.). (2014). *Agile Metrics—Lassen wir die Zahlen sprechen*. http://www.prowareness.de/wp-content/uploads/2014/10/whitepaper_agile_metrics.pdf.

Reich, A. (2021). *Was ist unter IP-Management zu verstehen?* www.dr-reich.com/wissenswertes/ip-management.

Council Directive 90/385/EEC of 20 June 1990 on the approximation of the laws of the Member States relating to active implantable medical devices, Pub. L. No. 90/385/EEC, 90/385/EEC 90/385/EEC (1990). https://eur-lex.europa.eu/legal-content/DE/ALL/?uri=CELEX:31990L0385.

COUNCIL DIRECTIVE 93/42/EEC of 14 June 1993 concerning medical devices, Pub. L. No. 93/42/EEC, 93/42/EEC 93/42/EEC (1993). https://eur-lex.europa.eu/LexUriServ/LexUriServ.do?uri=CONSLEG:1993L0042:20071011:de:PDF.

Sauerbrey, U., & Winkler, M. (2018). *Friedrich Fröbel und seine Spielpädagigik*. Fredinand Schöning.

Schastok, I., Munck, C., & Lill, P. (2018). *Steuerung agiler Teams und Organisationen: Kontinu ierliche Leistungssteigerung und Anpassungsfähigkeit sicherstellen* (pp. 177–192).

Schmid, A. (2019). Wirksames Projektcontrolling in Digitalisierungsprojekten. *Controlling, 31*, 47–53. https://doi.org/10.15358/0935-0381-2019-1-47.

Schmitt, M. (2013). Projektbewertung mit der Kapitalwertmethode. In A. Klein (Ed.), *Investment and Project Controlling* (pp. 105–123). Haufe.

Schopka, K. (2015). Controlling von hybriden Projekten—Herausforderungen und Chancen. In M. Engstler, M. Fazal-Baqaie, E. Hanser, M. Mikusz, & A. Volland (Eds.), *Projektmanagement und Vorgehensmodelle 2015* (pp. 183–187). Society for Informatics e. V.

Schreckeneder, B. C. (2013). *Projektcontrolling—Projekte überwachen, steuern, präsentieren* (4th ed.). Haufe. https://shop.haufe.de/prod/projektcontrolling-buch.

Schuh, G., Arnoscht, J., & Schiffer, M. (2012). Innovationscontrolling. In G. Schuh (Ed.), *Inno vationsmanagement: Handbuch Produktion und Management 3* (2nd ed., pp. 249–349). Springer Vieweg. https://doi.org/10.1007/978-3-642-25050-7.

Schwaber, K., & Sutherland, J. (2020). *Der Scrum Guide—Der gültige Leitfaden für Scrum: Die Spielregeln*. https://scrumguides.org/download.html.

Sellinger, K., Thomaschewski, D., & Völker, R. (2020). Agilitätsmanagement und Agilität im Controlling. In R. Gleich (Ed.), *Controlling Challenge 2025—Agile, Digital, Effective* (pp. 27–40). Haufe. https://shop.haufe.de/prod/controlling-challenge-2025.

Ulrich, P., & Rieg, R. (2020). Agilität in Projektmanagement und Projektcontrolling—Ergebnisse einer empirischen Studie. *Die Unternehmung, 74,* 187–215. https://doi.org/10.5771/0042-059X-2020-2-187.

Vahs, D., & Burmeister, R. (2005). *Innovationsmanagement: Von der Produktidee zur erfolgreichen Vermarktung (2005)*. Schäffer-Poeschel.

REGULATION (EC) No. 765/2008 OF THE EUROPEAN PARLIAMENT AND OF THE COUNCIL on the rules for the accreditation and market surveillance relating to the marketing of products and repealing Regulation (EEC) (2008). https://eur-lex.europa.eu/legal-content/DE/TXT/?uri=CELEX:32008R0765.

Regulation (EU) 2017/745 of the European Parliament and of the Council of 5 April 2017 on medical devices, Pub. L. No. (EU) 2017/745, (EU) 2017/745 (2017). https://eur-lex.europa.eu/legal-content/DE/TXT/?uri=celex%3A32017R0745.

Wanner, R. (2018). *Scrum—Agiles Projektmanagement und Scrum erfolgreich anwenden*. DASsachbuch.

Wobser, G. (2022). *Agiles Innovationsmanagement: Dilemmata überwinden, Ambidextrie beherrschen und mit Innovationen langfristig erfolgreich sein* (1st ed.). Springer Gabler. https://doi.org/10.1007/978-3-662-64515-4.

Wurzer, A. J., Grünewald, T., & Berres, W. (2016). *Die 360° IP-Strategie*. Franz Vahlen GmbH.

Zirkler, B., Nobach, K., Hofmann, J., & Behrens, S. (2019). *Projektcontrolling: Leitfaden für die betriebliche Praxis* (1st ed.). Springer Gabler. https://doi.org/10.1007/978-3-658-23714-1.

7 Afterword

When the authors decided to write this book together, they were able to draw on many years of expertise and experience in the construction of devices, teaching and further education, as well as business management control.

From this, they realized that:

- firstly, for their own professional work (and incidentally also for private life), the competence must be available to think creatively and develop innovative solutions and implement them practically, and
- secondly, their own methodological experiences should be conveyed to project members as well as to students and specialists and executives in professional further education.

For the methodological guidance, countless recommendations and instructions are available. The authors' work has shown that easily understandable, manageable, and practically prepared material is useful for the innovation process.

We have therefore tried to advance, from our point of view, to the core of creative work and to show that invention and innovation can be based on a few basic methods.

We hope that we have succeeded in doing this sufficiently, and that you as a reader and user have been able to gain the best possible insights and will continue to do so.

We would be delighted to hear an "echo" from you and for you to stay in dialogue with us in the future.

E. Busch et al., *Methodology of Innovation*, Contributions to Management Science,
https://doi.org/10.1007/978-3-658-50010-8_7

MIX
Papier aus verantwortungsvollen Quellen
Paper from responsible sources
FSC® C105338

If you have any concerns about our products,
you can contact us on
ProductSafety@springernature.com

In case Publisher is established outside the EU,
the EU authorized representative is:
Springer Nature Customer Service Center GmbH
Europaplatz 3, 69115 Heidelberg, Germany

Printed by Libri Plureos GmbH
in Hamburg, Germany